HURRICANE HELENE: RESILIENCY AFTER THE STORM

Part One

By Rebecca Wells Phillips

A portion of the book proceeds will be given to Hurricane Helene victims.

ISBN: 979-8-99942850-9 (Hardcover)
ISBN: 979-8-99942851-6 (Paperback)

Printed by Shaw Publishing in the United States of America.

First printing: August 2025.

Shaw Publishing
76 Arlene Drive
Belmont, NH 03220
www.shawhillpublishing.com
admin@shawhillpublishing.com

Definitions

CATEGORY 5 HURRICANE:
1. A tropical cyclone with winds exceeding 155 miles per hour, thus leading to extensive damage and destruction of buildings.

TROPICAL STORM:
2. A tropical cyclone with prolonged winds ranging between 39 and 73 miles per hour, with strong winds developing in tropical waters.

MUDSLIDE:
3. A large mass of wet earth that moves down a slope, also called mudflows or debris flows. A type of landslide occurs when heavy amounts of precipitation saturate soil, rock, and debris.

FLOOD:
4. The ability of something to return to its original size and shape after being compressed or deformed.

FEMA:
5. The Federal Emergency Management Agency responds to disasters declared by the President and provides financial assistance to individuals and households.

RESILIENCY:
6. The ability of something to return to its original size and shape after being compressed or deformed.

7. An ability to recover from or adjust easily to adversity or change.

POTABLE WATER:

8. Water that is safe to drink. It can be consumed directly or through food preparation.

FOREVER CHEMICALS:

9. Per- and Perfluoroalkyl substances (PFAS) are man-made chemicals that stay in the environment and human bodies for thousands of years due to their resistance to breakdown.

Merriam-Webster Dictionary[i]

Content Warnings

This is a historical collection of Hurricane Helene events. Please be aware of the following topics:

- Discussions of human and animal deaths

- General listing of missing people

- Detailed timeline of events

- In-depth interviews with victims

- Photographs of flooding and destruction

- Self-harm event and mental health discussion.

Table of Contents

Dedication

Following the horrendous events of Hurricane Helene, I had planned to include a list of people and pets lost during the storm however, my neighbors helped me realize that (1) I shouldn't profit from the loss of another person, (2) Doing so would require approval from families to publish victim names, and (3) this book is more about what went wrong during a catastrophe and how can we be better prepared in the future. With that out of the way, I do want to extend my deepest apologies to the families and friends deeply affected by the loss of their loved ones, including pets and livestock. Additionally, people remain missing, and there are people whom we may never find. Sadly, people from the homeless community and the undocumented, due to their illegal status, may never be known. I, again, am so sorry for the loss of these individuals because their families may never even know what has happened to them.

I would also like to thank all the first responders (police, firefighters, security, and civilians) who risked their lives saving others. Many of them lost their lives, and we will never be able to thank them enough for their sacrifice. When the rest of us are running away, these individuals are running into the fire, not even considering the risks they take with their lives. Yes, many have chosen the service profession, but none are expected to perish, especially during a tropical storm in the mountains.

Please join me in a moment of silence for these victims and their families. We will be stronger TOGETHER, but we will also never forget our lost friends and neighbors. God bless us all!

"SOUNDS" by Anja Woody

It's a pleasant fall evening here in the mountains.

21 DAYS

21 days since Helene changed our lives forever.

I went for a walk in my neighborhood. I noticed the sounds. Sounds of the crickets, dry leaves blowing across the pavement, dogs barking. These sounds have now mostly replaced other sounds that became commonplace after Helene. For days and days, there were sounds of helicopters traversing the sky - multiple times a day - from every direction -for days and days. Helicopters, sirens, generators - sounds once rare, now constant.

My thoughts with every siren I heard – what will they find – will they save someone – can they?

Now, so many stories, videos, and photos of destruction.

EVERYWHERE

Helene has robbed us, robbed us of our quaint small towns. Robbed us of what we once knew. Robbed us of our sense of community, our sense of security.

Hurricanes don't happen here.

Helene filled the rivers, streams, creeks, and culverts to more than anyone thought possible. She robbed people of their homes, their belongings, and their loved ones.

Large chunks of pavement, trees, trailers, homes, and cars tossed around like toys.

I was one of the lucky ones. I sit here in my home that now has power and water – although not drinkable – and I think how incredibly blessed and lucky I am.

But at times, the grief is overwhelming.[ii]

10-18-2024

Prologue

Close your eyes and imagine yourself sitting in your mountain home, watching television while the pouring rain dances on the windows and pounds on your roof. In an abrupt sequence of events, your power flickers off and on in a rhythmic light show of flashes until it finally fails, throwing you into a pitch-black abyss. Always prepared, you locate the flashlight with new batteries in your kitchen drawer and turn it on. With the sudden quiet from the power outage, you easily hear the heavy rain as it smacks and pounds your roof and windows. For the first time since the rain became deafening, you steal a glance out of the large pane window. As your mouth goes agape, your brain computes the reality of what you're seeing. A growing, foreign body of raging water resembling a tsunami engulfs your house and property. As you search the driveway, you search for the vehicle that has disappeared below the turbulent water.

Refocusing your attention inside your home, you glance down at the heavy oak front door and are shocked by the water appearing inside your once-safe abode. At this moment, horror grips you like someone choking the end of a water hose, and you know that your home has become your prison, and possibly your future coffin. As sweat begins beading on your forehead, your sweaty armpits emit an unfamiliar stench that you identify as fear. Now is not the time to chastise your decision to stay inside your home. Everyone had assumed you would be safe in a brick house on the top of the hill. The river below had always remained within its banks, and no one could have foreseen how much water would overtake the area. Unfortunately, the preceding rainy days delivered a deluge of water before Helene's arrival. To your amazement, Hurricane Helene was becoming much more destructive than any news media had forecasted.

Grabbing your cell phone to call for help, you are shocked to see that there is no signal and realize the phone is useless. Quickly, you walk into the kitchen to grab the cordless landline, only to remember that you'd canceled the service a couple of years ago when you needed to cut costs. Regret is a dead horse, and you decide not to revisit your decision because no one has landlines anymore. Just last week, you had the same discussion with your neighbor and now wonder whether his house beside the river survived the floodwaters. Thankfully, he had decided to stay with relatives in Arden, North Carolina, and not risk anything. Returning to the living room, you shine your flashlight on the floor and glimpse a small pond spreading into the living space.

Deciding to escape to higher ground, you grab your useless cell phone and run to the second floor. The master bedroom is at the end of the hall, so you hope you'll be safer there, but you can still hear the rushing water coming into your home. Slamming your bedroom door, your attention is grabbed by the sound of trees breaking in the distance. Pulling back the heavy curtains, you glance out the window and notice storm debris stacking up and hitting against the side of the house. Counting to ten and breathing slowly, you try calming your nerves, but it doesn't help. Unable to do anything, you lie on your bed and pray for the water to recede or the rain to cease.

As the hours pass, you keep looking at your phone, which only has 36% of its battery, and continue trying to make a call. Erroneously, you had believed a cell phone would always be reliable, no matter what the situation. When you purchased your phone, the service provider assured you that emergency or "SOS" calls would always work.

However, during an actual emergency, you want to scream at the loss of signal icon. Now, you notice the "SOS" letters on the screen, but you have no idea how to use the service. Excitedly, you finally remember that you can send SMS texts to your family and friends and ask them to send help. Unfortunately, when you attempt to text, you receive the error message, "Message failed."

Frustration overtakes reality, and you realize you are completely alone, forced to figure out a way to save yourself. Leaving the false safety of your bedroom, you investigate the water situation downstairs. Feeling a pang of hunger, you consider wading through the water to grab a snack from the kitchen to eat, foolishly berating yourself for not considering it sooner. With your flashlight in hand, you slowly walk to the stairs, only expecting to see a little more water on the first floor. However, as you get closer, the deafening sound of gushing water takes you by surprise. Directing the beam of light down the hallway, you are horrified to see that water is splashing against the top step of the second floor with branches, clothing, and other unknown debris. The odor of mud, gas, and chemicals emanates from the dark abyss. Abruptly, you turn around and sprint back to your prison, slamming the door and knowing there is no way out of this predicament. Lying down on your king-sized bed, you cry softly and say your prayers that no one will hear.

Following the days after Hurricane Helene ravaged the state of North Carolina, along with six other states, I was disheartened to read online comments such as, "Why didn't they leave?" and "How did they not know the storm would be so bad?" Perhaps these questions are just a way for people to blame the victims for their disastrous outcomes, naively thinking that any amount of preparation would have saved them from

11

the mudslides or flooding. Residing in the mountains of Tennessee and North Carolina, I am confident that everyone's last concern was evacuating their homes. If there had never been a need for people living a considerable distance from the waterways to evacuate, why would anyone feel the need to leave?

Flooding by the Rocky Broad River - Chimney Rock, North Carolina

In this painfully realistic situation, I want you to ask yourself the following questions. What would you do if you were faced with the same scenario? As you read the story above, did you blame the homeowner for not evacuating, or were you empathetic to their imminent danger? Were you frozen in fear as you relived and envisioned the unsettling event? Imagine the same story, but replace the water with a mudslide that suddenly appeared without warning in the dark of the night. Take away the flashlight and consider how most people aren't prepared enough to have a working flashlight. Imagine people hearing the rushing water surrounding them and unable to see the danger without a light source.

When living in the mountains, hurricanes don't concern anyone, and evacuating a home has never been necessary for individuals living far away from the waterways. As with what happened with Hurricane Katrina, many people in North Carolina lack the financial resources to escape a dire situation, even when given ample warning. Also, don't forget about the people who are sick, elderly, or disabled, who are barely hanging on to their livelihoods. In today's economy, people struggle to survive paycheck to paycheck, often lacking sufficient funds for necessities such as food, housing, and utility bills. Who can afford to pack up their belongings and escape to safety when it's never been necessary? Believe it or not, many commuters rely on bus transportation to get to their jobs, and during a hurricane, these services are often halted for the safety of both drivers and passengers. And without phone service, calling an Uber is out of the question.

French Broad River - Alexander, North Carolina

CHAPTER ONE

Storm of All Storms

"Hurricane Helene is ranked in the top 10 deadliest hurricanes."

CHAPTER ONE: The Storm of All Storms

Some events happen only once in a lifetime, if you're lucky, but some people now fear that this is only the beginning of the destruction we will experience from future storms due to climate change or global warming. Hurricane Helene swept into North Carolina as a powerful tropical storm that first materialized in the region on Friday, September 27, 2024. It looked as if an atomic bomb had been dropped. Helene caused Western North Carolina to suffer the loss of lives and property, thus destroying the idea that living in the Appalachian Mountains was a haven of safety. Ten days after the storm arrived, USA Today reported that Hurricane Helene is now ranked in the Top 10 Deadliest Hurricanes. [iii]

Various media platforms strongly urged the community to take the warnings seriously by purchasing bottled water, filling bathtubs and sinks with water, restocking batteries and non-perishables, and fully charging cell phones. Whether everyone followed those suggestions is doubtful, but just as in snowstorms, the bread and milk disappeared quickly from the grocery store shelves. However, unlike with the COVID-19 pandemic, toilet tissue aisles remained intact. *(Thank you for the small miracles.)* From what I've been able to ascertain, most people did not take the storm warnings seriously because Western North Carolina is too far inland to be affected by a hurricane. Everyone believes hurricanes only affect coastal regions, and tropical storms have only caused minor flooding in the past. Because of this belief, the public was wholly unprepared for the cataclysmic storm that brought us to our knees.

On Thursday, September 26, 2024, Hurricane Helene arrived in Florida's Big Bend area as a Category 4 hurricane. With its arrival, 800 miles of land experienced disastrous flooding and strong winds, resulting in countless power outages across the state.[iv] Western North Carolinians felt secure and protected by the surrounding mountains, which had always sheltered them from the worst storms and tornadoes. Sadly, no one could have predicted what was coming our way. Big Bend, Florida, was 652 miles from Asheville, North Carolina, and Western North Carolina continued life as usual.

Although heavy rains were forecasted for the Asheville area, communities were only concerned about the worrisome areas, as community leaders and first responders alerted them to the possibility of flash floods and potential evacuations. Natives of Asheville reminisced about the last significant flood, which claimed 80 lives in July 1916. On July 5, 1916, a Category 3 hurricane, called "The Gulf Coast Hurricane," visited Alabama. When it arrived in the Appalachian Mountains, heavy rain persisted for days. As if that wasn't bad enough, the Category 2 "Charleston Hurricane" slammed into Charleston, South Carolina, thus resulting in additional heavy rainfall and complete saturation in Western North Carolina. The "Great Flood" recorded flooding levels at 24.67 feet, but Hurricane Helene obliterated that long-standing record.[v]

No monetary amount or prayer could have prepared Western North Carolina for what Hurricane Helene unleashed on them. Rain totals throughout North Carolina ranged from 14 inches along the Blue Ridge Mountains, 31 inches in Yancey County, and 24 inches in Mitchell County. AccuWeather reported, "The original estimates of storm damage were $50 billion but have been updated to more than $225 billion."[vi]

The communities closest to the rivers were the first to lose their power. However, further away, communities lost their Internet connections, thus causing a common lifeline to valuable information, family, friends, and coworkers to disappear. Their inability to communicate with the outside world led to inaccurate reports of missing people, but this was the least of our worries following this storm.

Close your eyes and reminisce about when you were a child, and your family had a landline in your home. Do you ever recall a situation where your family lost the ability to make a phone call? Those were the good old days because no one was addicted to their phones, and life continued. If you couldn't call your best friend, you would hop on your bike and ride down the street to their house. Or your mom reassured you that you could try to reach them later. In the worst case, you had to wait until school the next day to tell your best friend whatever it was that you deemed so urgent the day prior. Now, with the luxury of cell phones, we expect to be able to reach anyone at any time, regardless of the weather or situation.

Following Hurricane Helene, the lack of communication presented many challenges for the affected counties in Western North Carolina. The fear of trying to contact a loved one, a friend, or another human being was indescribable. Your only option was to listen to the local news, returning to your vehicle occasionally for updates. They tell you that roads are washing away, or the flood level of this waterway is higher than ever before, and houses are washing away. Your mom lives next to that river, and you've been unable to reach her. Can you put into words what you are feeling at this very moment?

Marshall, North Carolina

Chimney Rock, North Carolina

What were you doing the day of the storm?

"I was hanging out at home with my two dogs, Smokey and Chaos, and trying to keep Smokey calm because he's scared of storms, and I was worried about my girlfriend because I couldn't get a hold of her. Didn't have any cell service or power. I tried to leave and go see her, but there was no way out. Every way I turned, it was either flooded or trees down."

Did you ever make it out of your area?

"Nope. I tried driving my old truck and then went back home and got my motorcycle, but it was about out of gas, and I still couldn't get around the trees, downed powerlines, or flooding."

How prepared were you for the storm?

"I wasn't prepared because I just figured we'd have a lot of rain. We've got a couple of ponds in my neighborhood, and I was shocked to see them flooding, but we'd had rain for two or three days before Helene."

What scared you the most about the storm?

"Not being able to get in touch with my girlfriend to make sure she was okay. A day or two after the storm, I had a friend who tried to help people, but the police weren't allowing them into the areas. He told me about seeing bodies in trees, and I just can't get that picture out of my mind."

<u>What lessons did you learn, or what do you want other people to know?</u>

"First, I will make sure that I have a full tank of gas in all my vehicles because we couldn't find gas for days after the storm. Second, I bought a generator because we were without power for so long. I'm thankful I live in a camper and cook on a grill most nights. And, third, I'll make sure to have plenty of dog food on hand because that was hard to find, too.

I need everyone to know that a hurricane is no joke. It doesn't matter where you live, it can destroy everything. I don't care if you want to call it Hurricane Helene or Tropical Storm Helene, it's all the same. As far as I'm concerned, I will always call it Hurricane Hell because I've never seen anything like it in my lifetime, and I pray I never see anything like it again."

Smokey Park Highway - Candler, North Carolina

<u>Tell me about your Hurricane Helene experience.</u>

"September 27, 2024, was the worst day due to Hurricane Helene. I'm from Swannanoa, North Carolina. We didn't think of preparing because of the past Hurricanes that only caused some flooding, but nothing like this. Flooding in Swannanoa was never this bad. No one was prepared for this type of flooding."

<u>Did you lose anything in the storm?</u>

"The only thing I lost personally was what was in my freezer and refrigerator. Residents closer to the river lost almost everything they had. Some people didn't lose as much as others. Houses were gone, and many lives were lost. The flood was estimated to be around 30 feet above the Beacon Bridge. Some businesses were gone. No matter how you think the next flood will be, it's best to be prepared even if it doesn't happen."

<u>Can you think of anything positive that came out of the storm?</u>

"The only positive thing I can think of is how the community rallied together to help out where it was needed."

<u>Do you plan to stay here?</u>

"Personally, I will stay in Swannanoa because I have lived here so long. I knew a lot of people who passed away from the storm. The water was so high that the only thing you could see was rooftops."

<u>Were you able to help anyone during or after the storm?</u>

"I live on the Old Highway 70 side of the Swannanoa River. I personally went down that way to see if there was any way I could help. When I got as far as I could go, it was devastating to see. Cars, utility trailers, 20 and 40-ft containers were going down the river, which had completely covered the roads. As far as I could see, there was nothing but water. No power, no drinkable water, no cell service for days to come. People on the Old Highway 70 side of the river had no way to get out, and no one could get in until Saturday, the 28th, and that was only by UTVs [Utility Task Vehicles] or boat."

Beacon Village - Swannanoa, North Carolina

Old Highway 70 at Owen Middle School - Swannanoa, North Carolina

Old Highway 70 (above F & J Store) - Swannanoa, North Carolina

F & J Food Mart on Old Highway 70 (next day) -
Swannanoa, North Carolina

Old Highway 70 - Swannanoa, North Carolina

Old Highway 70 (above convenience store) - Swannanoa, North Carolina

Old Highway 70 (above convenience store) - Swannanoa, North Carolina

CHAPTER TWO

An Ocean in the Mountains

"I've never seen anything like this in my entire life."

CHAPTER TWO: An Ocean in the Mountains

Before making Asheville home, my spouse and I narrowed our relocation options to the mountains or the coast of North Carolina. However, we promptly and easily decided on the mountains because we spent our childhoods growing up in Tennessee. We also discussed my fear of hurricanes, which scares me to death, much like the earthquakes in California. I questioned how anyone could decide whether to stay or leave in a hurricane. I wondered how employers felt about employees who chose to escape a storm that may or may not destroy everything around them. I didn't want to have to decide whether to leave during a hurricane, so I figured the mountains were much safer. I couldn't fathom dealing with my employer and possibly losing my job whenever I fled the inevitable coastal storms. After much discussion, we ultimately decided to return to the safety of the mountains. After raising our daughter in the Greensboro, North Carolina, area, we felt we were being called back to the more familiar mountains. We were looking forward to returning to a place like our Tennessee hometowns. However, life has a way of throwing a wrench into the best-made plans.

The Cliffs at Walnut Cove (before Helene) - Arden, North Carolina

With our technological advancements, people rarely consider the possibility of losing all communication or the Internet for an extended period. Internet outages are a normal aspect of life, but no one could have imagined how being without communication for weeks would affect people during a natural disaster. Anxious Western North Carolina communities were unprepared for the lack of Internet in the affected areas, which was detrimental in many ways. Without access to the Internet, no one knew who was dead or alive, whether anyone was helping those stranded by the raging floodwaters, or how bad the situation was after the storm finished destroying everything in its path. Emergency responders couldn't identify who needed assistance without reliable communication until they drove upon stranded vehicles on flooded streets or those buried underneath fallen trees. The US Federal Communications Commission reported, "As of Oct. 6 – more than a week after Helene made landfall – Mitchell County, North Carolina, still had 50% of cell sites out of service, while Yancey County had 72% of cell sites out of service."[vii]

Olivette area off Macedonia Street - Asheville, North Carolina

After spending days immediately following the hurricane checking on neighbors and asking people what they had endured, I was amazed at how many older community members said they'd never lived through anything like this before. They'd reminisce about the 1916 flood, either because of stories they'd heard from their relatives or recent news stories they'd watched on television, since Hurricane Helene had changed so many of our lives. The same comment was repeated: "I've never seen anything like this in my entire life."

The truth is that no one has ever expected to see such destruction from the torrents of water that gushed in and out of our cities, towns, and neighborhoods. I will never forget the sight of cars covered in water, knowing that rescue from the forceful water flow would be futile. The water moved like rapids, picking up automobiles, tractor-trailers, train cars, mobile homes, brick and stick-built homes, and people and carrying them away, never to be seen again. These memories are etched into my mind and deeply ingrained in my soul, and I pray that we never experience destruction like that of Helene again in my lifetime. However, there are no promises in life, and storms like these are becoming more common worldwide.

Flooding by the Broad River - Chimney Rock, North Carolina

Chimney Rock, North Carolina

Broad River - Lake Lure, North Carolina

Amboy Road - Asheville, North Carolina

Lake Lure, North Carolina

CHAPTER THREE

Unimaginable Flooding

"Families have resorted to living in tents and campers."

CHAPTER THREE: Unimaginable Flooding

Living in North Carolina, we acknowledge that some areas are prone to flooding, and we understand that it is a natural consequence of living near numerous rivers, lakes, and streams. However, it's different when areas that never flood are overwhelmed with torrential rains, powerful floodwaters, and deadly mudslides. The floodwaters lifted homes off their foundations, causing them to float down the river, much to the shock of unsuspecting residents and their neighbors. Unfortunately, the powerful force of the water continued to destroy the house by breaking it apart and depositing people into the raging torrent. Even an Olympic swimmer would have been ill-equipped to swim in the surging floodwaters, as it was responsible for dismembering its unsuspecting victims.

Previously, I was a tenant of The Groves at Towne Center in Fletcher, North Carolina. Flooding from the French Broad River was a regular occurrence around the road leading into Fletcher Park, located behind the apartment. Often, the park entrance and road to the park would be closed due to flooding, but water had never inundated the apartment units. However, Hurricane Helene was a different story when it created a massive lake in and around the apartments. Vehicles and all the first-floor apartments flooded due to torrential rains, forcing tenants to evacuate to higher ground. Asheville Citizen-Times reported, "At 6:04 pm on September 27, 2024, the Cane Creek River had hit 30 feet in the town of Fletcher…Residents were evacuated from the Groves at Towne Center Apartments in Fletcher."[viii]

Apartments Flooded by Cane Creek River –
Fletcher, North Carolina

River Arts District –
Asheville, North Carolina

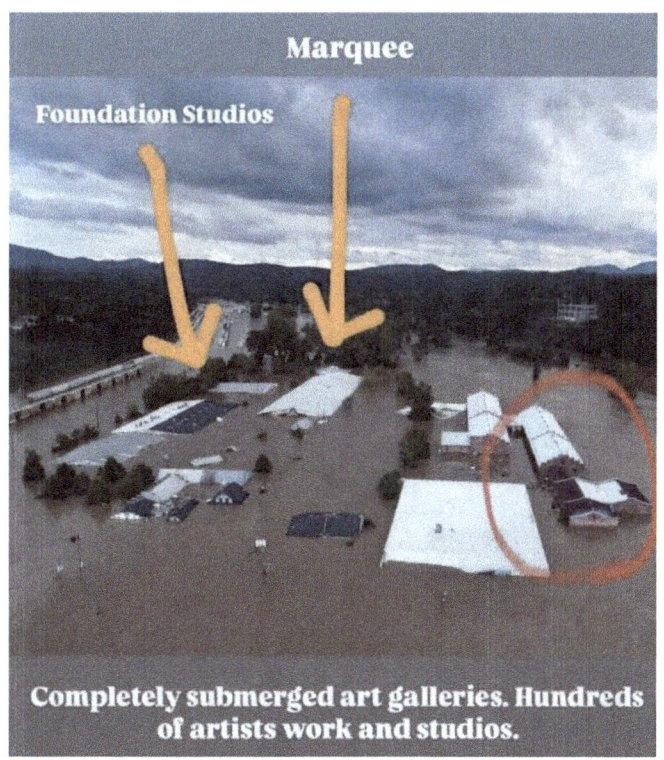

Tell me your Hurricane Helene story.

"Thursday was drizzly and grey, but I did not think too much about the incoming storm. I vaguely recall someone saying that Jim Cantore [from CNN Weather] was in town, and I kind of thought, 'Well, that can't be good!' My husband had colleagues from India in town, and we went to dinner with them, dropped them off at the Airbnb just down the road from us, and went home. My husband, Neil, was planning to drive them to the Charlotte airport the next morning. They had been in the United States for almost a month and were ready to return home.

I recall the torrential rain as I vaguely awoke around 1:30 am the morning of Friday, September 27, said a little prayer, and went back to sleep. Around 4:00 am, I heard the telltale signs of our power going out and listened intently for our generator to kick on. It never did, even though I had heard it run just days before. I did not think too much of it, but pulled the covers tighter as I heard the wind whip and tear through the trees. Around 6:00 am, we got up feeling a bit shaken. Both Neil and I reached for our cell phones to check on our son and his family, and his colleagues. There was no reception, no service whatsoever. Neil decided to get in his car and drive down to the Airbnb to check on the guys because they would be concerned about getting to the airport. As he left the driveway, his headlights hit the leaves of the massive oak that once stood at the top of our driveway. I felt a deep, devastating feeling in my gut. I saw him back up and go on the far side of the fence and drive away. Feeling a bit terrified, because of some PTSD from a windstorm at our other house, I prayed and sat down on our couch, watching the wind bend the trees in the back and sides of our yard. Just a few minutes

36

passed, and Neil walked back through the door. He was visibly shaken and told me that the road was completely impassable and there were massive oaks down everywhere. There was no drivable way out of our neighborhood. No way to check on the gentlemen from India, our son, or my mom.

Feeling completely helpless, I returned to my spot on the couch, worried and watching the wind, waiting for the next tree to fall. I made my other son come down the steps from his room above the garage because we have a huge oak tree standing near his room. A pop from the backyard and one of our oaks fell, snapped in half, and fell to the ground. Shortly thereafter, the far oak on the driveway popped and slid down the oak nearest the garage and Zachary's room. That tree stood firm, holding the other oak in its branches. To this day, I believe that my dad, who passed in August of 2022, was watching over us, and he held that tree up, so I did not fall on our house. There is no other explanation that makes sense in my mind.

Around 11:00 am or so, the winds began to subside, and the Carolina blue sky began to peek through. Neil, once again, got in his car and was going to try to make it to the guys from India to check on them, but there was not even a way to cut through the cattle field. He came back to the house and got Zachary and the little equipment we have, and went to help the neighborhood men cut a pathway to Cane Creek Road. Luckily, some of our neighbors have chainsaws, Bobcats, and other heavy equipment to help with this monumental task. Around 5:00 pm, they had cleared enough of a path to get a vehicle through, and Neil finally made it to check on the guys. These gentlemen from India had never experienced a hurricane or a storm of this caliber. Well, neither had we, but for them, it was totally out of the realm of anything they had experienced. Luckily, they had somehow been in touch with our son, Noah, and eased our minds about his safety.

After Neil got to them and they made a plan, he came back home and picked me up, and we loaded them up and began our journey to the Charlotte airport. It was getting quite dark by this time, and we were focused on getting them to the airport, so we did not witness the true devastation through Fletcher. We made our way to I-26 and about one mile toward South Carolina, traffic dead stopped. We witnessed cars turning around and people getting out of their cars and walking around. Finally, we crept up to the beginning of the line, and the guys told us that there were floodwaters over the wheel wells of the cars, and they advised us to turn around. They would not stop us from going through, but they warned us. Luckily, we have an SUV, and my husband was determined to get these gentlemen to their plane, so we pushed forward with angst and anticipation of driving through floodwaters. However, by the time we got to wherever those waters had been, it had receded, and we were beyond grateful.

Along I-26, we stayed in the left-hand lane because, randomly, there were trees down in the right-hand lane, and by this time, it was dark, with the only lights anywhere being the headlights of the few desperate cars on the interstate. At one point, this black car passed us flying in the right-hand lane. I did not get the words out of my mouth, 'You better slow down, or you are going to RUN INTO A TREE!' as he swerved in front of us to avoid a huge oak across the lane. Tears and adrenaline rushed through my body as I witnessed this chaotic driver being stupid!

Oh, I forgot to mention that September 27 is also mine and Neil's wedding anniversary, and this was our 27th year of marriage. We celebrated around midnight with a McDonald's Quarter Pounder and fries. That was also the first meal we had eaten that day, besides some snacks, as we navigated the aftermath of the storm. Arriving home around 3 am the morning of September 28, we fell into bed and had absolutely no idea of the utter devastation around us.

The next morning, Neil and Zachary went out to check on Neil's dad, who lives about seven miles from us. Every normal passage to Mr. Myers' home was decimated. Bridges washed out, powerlines down, and mudslides blocking the turns. They were gone for what seemed like forever, and I was getting worried. With no cell service, I could only wait for their return. When they finally got back home, I got a glimpse of the details of the utter devastation that ravaged our world. Then, when I ventured out to go check on my mom, I was addled by the staggering destruction I witnessed. Making it out to Leicester, I was awestruck by the lack of damage we found. So very grateful to find my mom's property to be perfectly fine, with water, power, and cell service intact. My family, my brother's family, and my sister's family found refuge in hot showers and potable water at my mom's house."

Did you do anything to help your community after the storm?

"When we found an evenness and got our power back, after about two weeks, I knew I needed to be out in my community helping in some way. My first assignment was with Samaritan's Purse. Approaching Swannanoa and Black Mountain felt ominous because I had heard, but not witnessed, the impact on this quaint mountain community. Tears filled my eyes as I drove through this area and seeing the horror that took place there. I made my way to the home I was assigned to and got my five-gallon bucket and shovel. The home I was working in was a good 1000 + yards from a wide creek bed that was at least 10 feet down. The flood line on the walls was at least four feet high, and six inches of mud lay on the floors. My heart was saddened as I removed cookbooks and memories from their pantry. The hardwood floors came up like spaghetti noodles that had been in the water too long. The fridge was left face down as the waters had rushed into the front door, swirled through the living room, and exited out the deck door. The backyard was littered with dishes and trinkets from the surrounding houses. I was in awe as I picked up a crystal dish, like the one I have of my grandmothers, without a chip in it. I left there exhausted, broken, but filled with hope as people from all over the country came to help their neighbors.

My second adventure into the abyss of devastation was in Burnsville. I rode up with my friend, Desiree, as she was going to work with AmeriHealth Caritas. The lady heading up the event had asked Desiree for a hot cup of coffee, but there was nowhere to get it. So, we stopped at a convenience store. As Desiree was microwaving bottled water to stir in some instant coffee, the cashier asked the elderly gentleman, maybe in his 80s, how he was doing. I heard the sadness and gratitude in his voice as he told her, 'I lost absolutely everything, and yesterday, they found a body on my property. But God is good.' I stood there with tears in my eyes and awe in my heart at the utter faith that this gentleman embodied.

My community, my home, of WNC, never ceases to amaze me. As the weeks have now turned into months, I have seen such utterly incredible resilience, humanity, selflessness, and inspiring miracles here in WNC. I have regained hope in humanity, in compassion, and a heart that is still incredibly prevalent in our world. Tears still come as I drive around and see empty lots where there used to be homes, restaurants and businesses."

What preparations did you make before the storm?

"Honestly, we did not prepare for this storm because we have a generator and were not greatly concerned. Just the fact that our generator decided not to work created issues that we weren't expecting, mostly the lack of access to water."

What did you lose in the storm?

"We lost six trees, three of those being mighty oaks. That is all the property we lost. But, for me, I lost a bit of security around our mountains. Having grown up here, it always felt safe and protected from destructive storms. But my dad had said, for years, that opening the mountains up to the four to six lanes of interstate would invite those storms in in ways we had never seen before. My dad was a brilliant man and could see things that others may not think about."

How are you managing after the storm? What provides your strength?

"During the storm, my strength came from prayer and the unity with my family. Also, keeping busy and offering help to my uncle, mom, and father-in-law gave us purpose when we felt we had no control over what was going on in our world. Today, my strength comes from witnessing the community that grew from this storm and the beautiful resilience of humanity."

What are your concerns right now?

"My concern right now is the mental and emotional well-being of the children of Western North Carolina. I do not think we have any idea of the remnants of PTSD that are living in their bodies, minds, and hearts. That is why I developed the "A Healing

Journey" journal for the youth of Western North Carolina and East Tennessee. If I can get these journals out to the kids, I believe it will help them process the vast impact that Hurricane Helene has had on all of us, truly. The fundraiser can be found at www.bethesparkmovement.com."

What message do you want to send to people?

"Resiliency is a given. As humans go through challenges, we can grow through these challenges. Once we come up for air, we can achieve and support each other through any threat or obstacle. Together, we are always stronger. Doing what must be done is a unique human ability to overcome and thrive on the other side of a disaster."

Can you name anything positive from this storm?

"Love, community, gathering, giving, selflessness, hope, humanity, and unity are all lessons and gifts from Hurricane Helene. I have great pride in the folks of Western North Carolina, East Tennessee, and the United States who came out to help their neighbors. I especially want to thank Tupelo Honey South, the Sheetz in Fletcher, and so many other local businesses that opened their doors to this community."

What makes you angry about what happened?

"Politics and how, no matter what, they can find a way to divide people. News coverage moving on so quickly is another sore spot. But that is not the humanity we needed anyway, so I push that nonsense aside and revel in the beautiful people who rolled up their sleeves and helped their neighbors."

Are you staying or leaving?

"I do not ever see myself leaving my lifelong home of Western North Carolina. Things can happen wherever we are, but not just anywhere is home."

Do you have any suggestions for the local or federal government or FEMA on how they responded to the storm?

"I definitely have some criticisms, because $750 is not even a drop in the bucket for what so many lost. There is always room for improvement when it comes to government and bureaucratic nonsense. Generally speaking, it is always the people who are selfless, kind, and compassionate who do the most for anyone in need. We need our government for many obvious reasons, but ultimately, it is the people who are going to hold you up when your feet no longer touch the ground. When we can acknowledge this and have gratitude for our fellow humans, is when the government and all their politics will become less important than being a good neighbor and creating a loving community.

These Mountains

Mother Nature
Hear our cries
You ripped our souls
We can't believe our eyes

The lands have shifted
The skies have opened
The waters raged
Left us lost and broken

Our mountains held
The best they could
But gave way, relenting
As waters grew to floods

Our houses shook
Our trees fought
Your strength proved more
Than anyone could have thought

Roots held on
With all their might
Timber grasping to stay
Tall and Upright

But, Helene, you were so mad
At what, we don't know
Taking out your fury
On our sacred land below

In your rage
You set to destroy and break
Leaving a path of destruction
In your wake

We've cried and mourned
We've hugged and scorn
Vowing to never let you win
We stood looking in the eye of your storm

Standing strong
As we dug from the rubble
Knowing you will not defeat
Those who stand humble

We will come back
Stronger than ever
These Mountains are different
Our community, you won't severe

So be assured
Miss Helene Hurricane
You had your rage
But these mountains
Will live to fight another day

~Carrie Myers
#WNCstrong

The swelling tsunami of rushing water destroyed numerous businesses throughout Western North Carolina. Additionally, many employees were now without a job, resulting in a rise in the unemployment rate for Buncombe County. In October 2023, the unemployment rate was 2.7%, the lowest in the state. However, the rates in October 2024 jumped to 8.8%, a remarkable increase in such a short time. Then, after Hurricane Helene, the unemployment rate dropped to 7.2. The Asheville metro area lost an estimated 8,000 jobs.[ix] Although most restaurants closed temporarily due to the lack of potable water or electricity, some restaurant owners decided to close their doors indefinitely, unable to see past the insurmountable odds of repairing their establishments. However, the operating restaurants could only offer bottled water, juice, or milkshakes with meals because of the lack of clean, potable water. Burger King had huge tanks of potable water brought to the parking lots of their establishments. Although water is now flowing into our homes and businesses, we've been instructed to avoid drinking it because of the numerous contaminants found within it.

Flooding by French Broad River - Asheville, North Carolina

A local who works closely with the Asheville Arts community mentioned that around 800 artists and musicians have left the River Arts District due to the numerous losses of artwork, inventory, supplies, and instruments. Many artists explained that they could not recover from Hurricane Helene and had to leave Asheville to find a new home for their talents.

CURVE Studios at 3 River Arts Place - Asheville, North Carolina

The owners of mobile homes previously placed in designated flood zones have been instructed to relocate their homes to a different location. This feat is only possible if the home survived the damaging water and mold. A search on Google.com discussed the lack of information about the number of mobile homes located in Asheville's flood zones, but assigned a 45% chance of flooding in general. Many families resorted to living in tents and campers due to the damage caused by Hurricane Helene, while they looked for permanent housing.[x]

On the night of the storm, Brother Wolf Pet Rescue of Asheville reported that 75 cats were displaced and went into foster homes due to the rising waters surrounding the business. To assist with pet evacuations, the Humane Society of Charlotte picked up 50 animals, transporting them to Charlotte, out of harm's way. Additionally, organizations such as Queen City Animal Hospital in Charlotte came to the rescue during this time of need. They used fundraisers to raise money to help provide the animals with food and supplies. Representatives reminded us that their work saves both the current animals and those in the future.[xi] However, there is no feasible way to track the number of rescued or homeless pets that were lost during the storm.

There have been multiple horrific stories shared about friends, families, and neighbors who were affected by Helene's floods. One story involved a man in Marshall, North Carolina, who watched his neighbor and dog float by while sitting on the roof of their house. The neighbor's body was found three days later, still holding his beloved pet in his arms. Miraculously, it was still alive. In another story, a mother tried to drive to safety with her infant buckled in the backseat, but a mudslide and rushing floodwater created a sinkhole where they were trapped and ultimately lost. Another mother lost her seven-year-old son after he was swept from her arms by the flooding.[xii].

Marshall, North Carolina

Brother Wolf Adoption Center - Asheville, North Carolina

Burton Street - Asheville, North Carolina

Chimney Rock, North Carolina

Following the torrential rainfall and associated mudflows, especially in areas near Interstate 40 between North Carolina and Tennessee, additional flooding occurred at the French Broad River, which regularly flooded Brevard Road and Biltmore Village. According to the North Carolina Medical Society and the National Weather Service, the rainfall between "Busick in Yancey County had 30.78 inches, Spruce Pine 24.12 inches, Hendersonville 21.96 inches, Mountain Home 17.09 inches, Candler 16.18 inches, Tryon 15.78 inches, Grandfather Mountain 15.42 inches, Highlands 14.86 inches, Banner Elk 14.85 inches, Mills River 13.26 inches, and Swannanoa 13.21 inches."[xiii]

The rainfall amounts have created a record that no one ever wanted to be broken, and people are now traumatized every time rain is in the forecast. I've spoken with multiple people, and we share the same anxiety when we hear rain hitting our roofs or slapping our windows. The additional fear of powerful wind gusts knocking over trees like sticks will continue to haunt us. Although Hurricane Helene has left us, our memories of what happened will stay with us forever, never giving us a moment of respite. Mudslides, fallen trees, flooded streets, and the smells of death and decay will remind us of what we have lost. People can rebuild homes and businesses, but the lives lost are irreplaceable. This won't be the first storm, nor will it be the last.

McDonald's at Biltmore Park - Asheville, North Carolina

J. Gabriel Boutique at Biltmore Park- Asheville, North Carolina

Alexander, North Carolina

Chimney Rock, North Carolina

CHAPTER FOUR

No Escape from the Storm

"I-26 and I-40 were so damaged that a large portion has fallen into the Pigeon River."

CHAPTER FOUR: No Escape from the Storm

Traveling in the area was treacherous and hopeless for many of us. I remember trying to get to my girlfriend in Candler, North Carolina, to ensure she was safe in her camper. As I continued my urgent journey, I searched aimlessly for roads that were clear of water, downed trees, fallen power lines, and abandoned cars. I'll never forget the frustration of trying for over an hour to get to her, only to finally give up and return to my home. After experiencing the absolute destruction of what Helene had done and being unable to confirm whether my friend was dead or alive, I spent the next day lying in bed in complete shock at the absolute devastation I'd witnessed.

Florida, North Carolina, South Carolina, Tennessee, Georgia, and Virginia suffered significant losses, including the destruction of many homes and bridges, resulting in the closure of approximately 400 roads deemed unsafe for travel. Parts of North Carolina saw 30 inches of rain, triggering flash floods and landslides. In Tennessee, the Kisner Bridge spanning the Nolichucky River collapsed. Five bridges were swept away, and 14 state highways were destroyed. The National Weather Service declared that additional landslides remained possible in portions of Western North Carolina communities. People trapped in their homes were without power and surrounded by flooding, fallen trees, and closed roads.[xiv]

Neighbors in Candler discussed the impassable roads and the frustration of not being able to reach loved ones by car or phone. Asheville residents crowded Leicester and Patton in search of potable water and food. People from different areas were trying to escape Western North Carolina in hopes of finding food, water, gasoline, and other essential supplies, but I-40 was impassable due to a mudslide. Every way we turned, there was an obstacle in our way. Screaming and crying did nothing but intensify the frustrations we were feeling inside our nightmare-like existence. We had never experienced such devastation and helplessness until now. Hurricane Helene destroyed us and our sense of safety. Our hopes crumbled along with the homes and businesses damaged in the storm. Tears streamed down our faces as we listened to the radio. Recounting what we had seen drove us to the brink of disaster. Wanting to run away from the pain, we were unable to find a clear path that would allow us to leave. Our beloved Western North Carolina had turned its back on us and let us down.

I-40 East Mudslide After Hurricane Helene

xv

"On the day of the storm, we were scheduled to work because everybody was a little lax about it, but as the day progressed, we started hearing that the water was rising, so my employer [Haywood Family Eye Care] closed. Around 10 am, my son Aizen was getting nervous, and my husband Travis was outside trying to clear out the culvert around the creek to keep the water from flooding near our camper. But he lost the shovel and almost fell into the rushing water, and decided to stop. Soon, there was a break around the creek, so Aizen and I crossed over and went to a friend's home on higher ground. Travis stayed behind with the two dogs, Zoe and Nezia, and fell asleep for an hour. In that hour, the water rose a foot above, so Travis barely made it over with the dogs. We couldn't get out of the area because of the flooding and trees, no cash, no nothing, and we weren't prepared."

Beaverdam Community - Candler, North Carolina

What happened after everything settled down?

"A couple of weeks later, we did 'primitive camping' where we had to prepare everything we were going to do before the sun went down. Dishes and laundry were done in the creek, and our water tank was filled from the creek."

Do you worry about other storms?

"Yes. When it rains, I get very nervous because of the past flooding. I get really nervous with a lot of rain and the trees falling. No one anticipated that, and that's even with me coming from Florida. I was shocked at how fast the rivers filled up. It was very different from storms in Florida because you didn't really have the wind, but that water was so fast, and it was very scary."

What scared you the most about the storm?

"Not being able to contact anyone for about a week. Everything was unorganized, and no one was ready for what happened at all. We asked opinions from people who had lived here their entire lives, and they warned us about letting the culvert get clogged, but said the water would never get to the camper. Afterwards, they apologized because what happened they had never been what they had experienced."

How did your son, Aizen, handle what was happening?

"He's pretty good at hiding his emotions, but he was nervous. He kept asking, 'Where's Travis, where's Nezia [a Doberman] and Zoe [a German Shepherd],' and asking me, 'Are you okay?' He was worried for sure."

What did your coworkers experience?

"We had a few people living in Waynesville who were pretty fortunate. There was one employee who was out of water for a long time, and she was in Asheville. We gathered a lot of supplies for her. She had no water, so people offered to let her wash her clothes at their houses. Our employer tried to help all of us. One person lost their entire home. For them, the practice [Haywood Family Eye Care] provided them with new eyeglasses for free."

Were there other ways or people who tried to help victims?

"Travis made some trips out. He went to Asheville to find someone who had a young infant, but Asheville was torn up. The water was still up. He and a friend went to Fairview, North Carolina, and that was very intense. Police wouldn't allow them to take a generator to anyone. They needed to take it to a family with a grandmother on oxygen. No explanation was given, but the police wouldn't let them pass. They considered driving around the police, but the truck was too heavy. Later, they heard a rumor, but I believe there were so many deaths and so many things that weren't appropriate for the public to see. I just didn't understand all the secrecy for no reason. Most people are not stupid and understand that what happened was very bad and that lives were lost. Seems like the police didn't want things on social media, such as showing deceased family members or their relative's destroyed home."

Do you think the secrets were beneficial for us?

"People outside of North Carolina felt like it wasn't a big deal because of that. My family knew because I was telling them everything, but other people didn't realize it was that bad. I even heard on the radio that a police chief or someone high up told the media that 'stealing is stealing.' See, there was a semi-trailer that had a bunch of water on it, and the officials weren't going to distribute the water until other supplies had arrived first. So, citizens started distributing the water, and an officer said he was going to arrest them for that. How are you going to get someone in trouble for trying to help your neighbors? Why would you call that stealing? I don't believe the citizens were doing anything wrong."

Was the government prepared for the disaster?

"The government was not organized at all. I understand that no one expected this. There was flooding back in Caruso, North Carolina and a trailer from the trailer park floated and butted up against the fire department, so they couldn't get out to rescue people. After something like that, shouldn't someone come up with a contingency plan? Our tax dollars pay you to make plans and keep us safe. How can you not have any plans? All we had to rely on was one radio station for updates. There needed to be more transparency. People were looting, but they were even more desperate because nothing was changing. I understand that you can't plan for everything, but you have to plan for something."

What advice do you have for someone to help them prepare for disasters?

"For me, I would say that the biggest thing for us was making sure you have water. If they [local officials] say it's going to be serious, heed that warning. We would have been way better off if we'd prepared better. Our neighbors were like a big community, and we, the people, stood up for each other and took care of each other. Have enough water and cash on hand because there is no electricity. For three people, I would suggest having at least $500 in cash if you are able and spend it sparingly. Have one case of water per person. If you can help someone, please do it."

<u>How did you handle all the food in your refrigerator or freezer without electricity?</u>

"Try to be neighborly and share your food. Our neighbors gathered all their food, and each night, we would take turns grilling and serving a smorgasbord of food for everyone to enjoy. Even if you're introverted like me, you must behave differently in situations like this.

Enka Lake Road at Sand Hill - Candler, North Carolina

Smokey Park Highway - Candler, North Carolina

The radio stations did their best to keep the community informed about what was happening in and around the aftermath of Hurricane Helene. We learned that there were 21 tornadoes in South Carolina, that 1.4 million people were without power, and that 48 people had perished in the state of South Carolina. On September 29, the flow rate of the French Broad River grew to a "rate of more than 240,000 gallons per second, enough to fill an Olympic-sized swimming pool every 2.74 seconds."[xvi] According to the USGS, Helene triggered more than 2,000 landslides, with the majority occurring in Western North Carolina. Major interstates I-26 and I-40 were so damaged that a large portion near the state line with Tennessee fell into the Pigeon River. Interstate 40 is a major connection between North Carolina and Tennessee, and it is the most common route through the Southern Appalachian Mountains. Its average daily traffic of 26,000 vehicles and 7,610 trucks illustrates how essential I-40 is to the surrounding communities and states of California, Arkansas, Tennessee, and North Carolina. This lifeline was closed at the state line due to a mudslide caused by Hurricane Helene, resulting in a partial collapse of the interstate.[xvii]

While driving into unexpected barriers of water, trees, and power lines, I soon realized I was rapidly emptying my half-full tank of gas. The scenes reminded me of an apocalyptic movie. Due to a power outage, some service stations were unable to pump gasoline from their underground holding tanks. As if the situation wasn't bad enough, the stations fortunate to have power were increasingly faced with overly eager customers filling their cars' tanks to the brim and pumping gasoline into multiple gas cans. Western North Carolina had fuel shortages for days before finally allowing the purchase of a mere $20 worth of gas at the local Ingles grocery store. Ironically, the Ingles gas station had

90,000 gallons of gas delivered to their underground tanks before the storm hit, but when the power was lost, there was no viable way to pull the gasoline from the underground tanks. Once the electricity was restored, customers were limited to purchasing $20 worth of gas at a time. Other gas stations followed with their restrictions to ensure that there was enough gas to go around, but some of us were still unable to find gas for a few days following the storm.

Gas Stations throughout Western North Carolina

What were you doing the day of the storm?

"That morning of the storm, at 8 am, I was down at the brewery, and we had closed the day before because the [Rocky Broad] river was getting crazy, but we were used to that. It was about a foot over our lower deck. I had no idea how big this thing would be and took a video saying, "The worst is yet to come, and I never realized that the worst would be what it ended up being. It had rained for almost two or three days prior to the storm getting here. We went to bed, and I had cameras at the brewery and had a kegerator, which is a refrigerator that holds four kegs of beer so that people don't have to lug it down the stairs, and we'd just invested in this thing. I was watching the cameras as the water was rising, and it was about 1 to 1 ½ feet away from that kegerator, and then the power went out. That was probably a good thing."

Chimney Rock Brewing's Camera Shot – Chimney Rock, North Carolina

"Woke up next morning, and it was calm, raining, and we had no power. I got a generator going, but Lake Lure didn't even have a tree down on our street. Saturday morning, I told my wife, 'Let's go out and see what's going on.' I drove my truck down the road and left Lake Lure, and looked down into the lake, and it was up 10 feet to the top of the boat houses. We drove around the town center of Lake Lure, and there were wires and trees down. It was ghostly. Got down to Flowering Bridge, and it was piled with 30 feet of debris, trees, propane tanks, wash machines, freezers, and I couldn't go any further to get into Chimney Rock unless I climbed over that. The Bridge was still there, but water had dug all the dirt out from around it and eroded 50 yards of dirt out of there. Looked like another planet."

Flowering Bridge – Lake Lure, North Carolina

"It was another week before we could even get into Chimney Rock. My daughter lives about six hours away, and when I finally got to speak to her, she asked me if I'd gotten into Chimney Rock, and I told her no. She said, 'Well, Dad, it's gone.' I said, 'You mean all the decks are gone?' She then said, 'No, Dad, the brewery is gone.'"

<u>Were you shocked that your daughter knew about it before you did?</u>

"It was ironic that my daughter was the one to tell me when she's six hours away in New Jersey. It was incomprehensible. Nobody ever loses an entire building. It was mind-blowing to see the whole strip of businesses and seven other businesses gone. When we got there, we had no conception of where they [the businesses] were. The river was in a completely different place and went up Main Street. Our whole strip was just gone; not even the concrete slab was there. That was the first week, I guess."

Chimney Rock Brewing Co. – Chimney Rock, North Carolina

<u>What were the other businesses that were washed away with yours?</u>

"Restaurant Highlands had just relocated and had only been open one year. All the buildings were old and from the 1970s. A Mexican restaurant called La Montana, a

Hershey's ice cream store, a coffee shop [Coffee on the Rocks], an old-time photo shop, and Old Rock Café."

Were any other bridges affected by the flooding?

"Every other bridge got taken out. State Park Bridge and all bridges got taken out except for Flowering."

What are you going to do for work now?

"This was a retirement job for me. I'd been at the same company for 44 years in Charlotte, and we would always vacation here. My wife has some health issues, so it was a great fit, and we had a great team here, and it was good for us. The other businesses were dependent on the businesses for money and lived month-to-month. The owners of the coffee shop lived behind the shop. He told his wife to get out now because she was trying to gather up stuff. She got out just in time when the water took the shop, their home, all their belongings, and even their cat. It was a devastating loss. September 27th is the kick-off for leaf season, and businesses need that money to get through the Fall and Winter. The other businesses that were still standing took on three to four feet of mud and are trying to open by Memorial Day weekend, but the entire sewer and water systems got washed out and probably wouldn't be here until August or September, so I don't know.

Are you rebuilding the business and staying in Chimney Rock?

"At this point, my quick answer is, I don't think I'm going to rebuild, especially not where we were. The storm carved the road and is 10 feet lower, and really in a flood zone now. If we could rebuild, the building codes are going to be crazy. We'd have to find other land. It's probably going to be a store pop-up here and there. There were eight eating and drinking places, and there are going to be only two now. I don't know when the park is going to open. Lake Lure cross-pollinated with Chimney Rock because we had the Beach and the lake, which are now off limits. We do have our brewery in Mars Hill in the 1947 movie theatre, but Mars Hill isn't Chimney Rock. 90% of our business was in Chimney Rock. Mars Hill isn't a big touristy area. I'm just taking it one day at a time. The state has a mitigation program where they supposedly will offer the business owner money for the value of the business before the storm. If we take it, they'll turn it into green space forever, which I think is what everyone else did. The magic of the place was that we were on the river. We were 10 days shy of our two-year anniversary and had planned a big event for that. It's sad for the whole area. I watch and read everything about all the other towns that have suffered what we've suffered."

How are your employees?

"We had seven employees in Chimney Rock, and we had the best staff in the whole town because they were all there all the time. Not transient, we had employees who were with us 3, 4, 5, 6, 7 years. Most of them were semi-retired, and I see them all the time. They're all alive and well. One employee lost her parents' 1940s house when a giant tree fell on it and destroyed it. Our GoFundMe page really helped everyone out, but it's closed now. My daughter started it right out of the gate, and it was overwhelming how much money we got in it, but we shut it down so that people could give to other people. People all over the country loved coming to our place. We're now making donations to other people with those same funds."

What preparations did you make before the storm?

"We always did the same things. We have three decks, and one is 10 inches below. We removed all the furniture and brought it to higher ground. We had a pop-up tent; we took it down and battened everything up. The funny story is that in the summer, we only have one bathroom, so we get a nice port-o-john, but the guy who owned that company said he wanted to come get it. He said that you never know after the 1994 flood, and that thing costs $1500 to make. I said that the river is 20 feet below it, but we'll need it for an event the next weekend. I should have listened to him. We did the normal prep for 3-4 feet only. It was unfathomable that the water was so high and so wide."

Chimney Rock, North Carolina

Chimney Rock, North Carolina

Rocky Broad River - Chimney Rock, North Carolina

<u>What do you think is responsible for destroying your business?</u>

"These bridges are going down the river, you're driving along the river the entire

time. The river is raging and water is coming down from tributaries and wiped out Bat

Cave, all the debris comes down and damns up at the bridges. The covered bridge in Bat Cave was the closest, and it was built up and finally broke. I think that is the tsunami or wall of water that came down, and it happened in like an hour. My friend walked his dog at 6:30 [in the morning] on Flowering Bridge, and it was an hour later that the water came and started flooding. It happened quick and was over quick. It was just devastation. I've had six months and am drained of emotion now. I've driven through Bat Cave and know this place like the back of my hand, but now, if you blindfolded me and dropped me in there, I wouldn't know where I was."

Have you heard any stories about the devastation in Bat Cave?

"Yeah, a Tiki bar got completely washed away. My friend saw headlights coming down the river. He was staying at the hotel. He said, 'I see headlights, and there's a car going down the river.' When it passed, he saw a woman with her hands on the window as it passed by. He still probably has PTSD about that."

Are you planning to stay here or leave?

"There's still destruction, and other new businesses are coming up, but it's going to be years before Chimney Rock comes back up. We're not going anywhere. We love it here and love the people. We're originally from New Jersey. The first chance we got to retire, we came here."

Do you have any advice for people or businesses regarding future storms?

"No, it's easy to sit back and say we should have been more prepared, but we couldn't have prepared for our building to be washed away, along with seven other businesses. No one expected it to be like this. There were no warnings saying the water was coming up 30 feet. Our lake filled with everything we used to live in or with."

Lake Lure Washburn Marina - Lake Lure, North Carolina

How can people help Chimney Rock or Lake Lure?

"Every single restaurant in Lake Lure, 13 places, are open, and the best thing you can do is take a ride out, have coffee, have dinner, stay the night. They're dying for business. Sympathy tours are probably going to help, and maybe staying for a week. Zipline, horseback riding, and hiking trails are opening. There are so many opportunities for giving money. BeLoved Asheville makes sure the money gets into the hands of people who need it. Riverside Stables is open for horseback riding. We have four wineries about 20 minutes away. Columbus has a brewing company. Tryon Equestrian Center is like a big horse world. It opened space for businesses to set up for free until April 1st. They have a big entertainment center with pool tables and darts."

Do you think Chimney Rock got the worst of the storm?

"It's a small town, and then when you wipe out half the businesses, it has a huge impact. Chimney Rock was an intimate time where it was like a walk back in time. We barely had the Internet. It [Chimney Rock] tugged on people's hearts. I think that's why it seems like Chimney Rock had it worse. We lost all the buildings, whereas Marshall had their water recede, and the buildings are still there."

Chimney Rock State Park – Chimney Rock, North Carolina

Chimney Rock, North Carolina

CHAPTER FIVE

Perilous Situation

"The soles of my boots came apart because of the chemicals in the water."

CHAPTER FIVE: Perilous Situation

As people's tempers heightened, everyone was terrified of the unknown and the lack of communication from the outside world. In one day, there were three shootings: two at a gas station and one at a fast-food restaurant in Candler, North Carolina. One of the murders was because someone jumped in front of someone in the gas line, and a man pulled out a gun and shot that person dead. There were multiple looting events where people were stealing from stores and gas stations and breaking into homes. In a horrific turn of events, one family escaped to South Carolina during the storm and returned later to their ransacked house. Not only did the flood destroy property, but vandals contributed by stealing precious belongings. Another family in South Carolina escaped their home when a tree fell on it during the storm. They had kept a generator running to keep the lights on so people would think someone was living in the home. However, someone first stole the generator, and then someone else stole family heirlooms and an antique rifle.[xviii]

With the loss of power, grocery stores suffered the loss of perishable items, particularly frozen foods, meats, and dairy products. When stores reopened, they had to limit the number of customers allowed inside due to concerns about looting and reduced product selections. I stood in line for forty-five minutes to buy only a few food items and charcoal for grilling. A bag of ice was almost $4, but it was necessary to keep my purchases from spoiling. I also spoke to a neighbor who said they went to a local convenience store and paid $75 for about four items, one of which included Tums and non-alcoholic items. Price gouging during a disaster is illegal, but that didn't dissuade some businesses from taking advantage of the perilous situation. North Carolina's

Attorney General Josh Stein reported that the Department of Justice had received 308 complaints alleging price gouging. The most common complaints originated from groceries, hotels, and gas stations, with a majority concentrated in Buncombe, Henderson, and Cleveland counties. Residents were encouraged to report price-gouging events to www.ncdoj.gov/pricegouging or 1-877-5-NO-SCAM.[xix]

Dealing with such a dire situation reminded me of the movie *The Purge*, in which citizens had a free-for-all for one day and could do whatever they wanted. Never in my imagination would I have considered anyone in Western North Carolina desperate enough to kill another over gasoline or steal from an empty house. Until you find yourself in a similar situation, you won't know what you're willing to do when you need essentials. Survival of the fittest becomes the mantra whenever people are in desperate situations. I do not judge others for their decisions, but it saddens me to think that people in Western North Carolina had to take from others to survive.

Hundreds of people are currently homeless due to the loss of their homes. One person has been living in a hotel and her car since the storm due to her inability to pay her rent, and the apartment evicted her, along with her partner and two children. I'm not sure what the answer is for the homeless situation because the problem has existed for years. However, I never could imagine the heartlessness of a landlord evicting a family during the worst natural disaster in years. I understand that businesses have expenses and need to make a profit, but I don't know why the government didn't intervene to keep people off the streets.

Everything that happened during Hurricane Helene was an anomaly, and no one understood how or why it occurred in that manner. The massive amount of rainfall before the storm was also unusual for that time of year. This is why some people have developed their conspiracy theories for that day's events, which led me to speak with a Candler local about her experience with the storm.

What were you doing the day of the storm?

"I worked that day. I do asphalt work. It didn't hit till later in the day. That night, I didn't realize it'd done anything until I saw the creek was rising over the road, and we had five ways out of here and couldn't get out. All the trees were down, mudslides, and everything else."

Where did you go to help people?

"When we finally could get out, we went and tried to help whoever we could. Down off North Fork in Black Mountain, which goes into Swannanoa, people were stuck there. They'd gotten out as the water came into the trailer park, but when they got back, there was nothing there."

Have you ever experienced so much destruction?

"No, I'd never seen anything like this before. I think they [the government] left the dams open too long, and then they couldn't shut them down in time. The dams were open for too long. There's one dam in Black Mountain and then there's another one in Bee Tree, and it's very bad around the dams."

Have you seen around the dams?

"Yes, we're redoing the pavement there. There's nothing there. One damn on Enka Lake Road in Enka, was emptied out [lowered] before the storm even hit."

Are you from this area?

"Born in New York, but I was raised in Black Mountain and have been here since I was age 3."

How did your family come out of the storm?

"Billy [husband] and I had a lot of family that was washed out, especially the ones in Old Fort. A lot of guys at work had their houses completely buckled in; my boss in Waynesville had the same thing happen. Some other guys were living in trailer parks down in Canton, and it was bad."

Do you have any advice for people?

"Make sure you know how to take care of yourself in case you don't have anything like lights, water, or the necessities. If you're going to buy property, make sure it has a small river or something so you'll have access to water to flush toilets and drink. Yeah, it's at risk of flooding, but it's your lifeline. You can't feed animals without water or grow your gardens without water."

Can you think of one positive from the experience?

"People. Just people came together and helped each other. By Ingles warehouse, one truck got stuck in the woods, and people went down there and realized there was water inside the truck, and started pulling it out and setting the water out by the side of the road for people in need. There was no clean water, there still isn't."

<u>Was there anything that scared you about what's happened?</u>

"Yes, when we were helping, the soles of my boots came apart because of the chemicals in the water. Just recently, they pulled the last semi-truck out of the river within the last month. It's been sitting there for months in the French Broad River, which comes directly through Swannanoa. When they tried opening the North Fork Dam, it did some damage, and it broke around it. They [the government] weren't prepared for their actions. I don't think this was just nature. When you mess with our climate, God's gonna get you. You're playing with fire, and a lot of people have died."

<u>Do you think we'll ever know exactly how many people perished in this storm?</u>

"No, we won't know how many died. They [the government] had hundreds of FEMA refrigerated trailers, and it was supposed to be for bodies. Why do you have hundreds of them if you don't have that many bodies? As thick as the sand and dirt is, there's no way to know. And no one can count the number of homeless people who may have washed away."

<u>Do you have any advice for the government?</u>

"Yeah, leave our stuff alone and stop messing with our climate. One minute they say it's too dry, and the next time it's too wet. God always makes a way. Also, we had a lot of flyovers just before the storm hit, and a lot of people noticed it. We're not dumb. We were able to take care of ourselves, and the communities came together like ours and did what we had to."

Shumont Road – Black Mountain, North Carolina

CHAPTER SIX

How Bad Is It?

"Twenty-six days later, and we're still working to restore utilities to everyone."

CHAPTER SIX: How Bad Is It?

When communication was working again, I received text messages from friends asking whether Asheville and the surrounding areas were as bad as the news had reported. My response every time was, "Yes. It's really bad." At that point, I hadn't realized how bad it was, and still is, in Western North Carolina. The rumor mills and lines of misinformation were working overtime as people lost their homes, businesses, and lives. Without access to the Internet or news, we relied on local radio stations to fill the void and help us feel normal again. We didn't learn about the lies and false information circulating until days after the storm hit. Believe it or not, it took me a couple of weeks to get reliable Internet service, but others weren't as fortunate. Customers were unprepared for the substantial damage to Spectrum's physical infrastructure and the non-functioning Internet service in areas around Asheville. "Network hubs require power to deliver service to nearby areas, meaning that even if an area has power, some in that same area may still be without service if outages in that area are still active."[xx]

The circulating rumors complicate matters even further, but when people speak the truth about what is happening, they're accused of being overly dramatic and exaggerating to gain attention. One story described a scene with bodies stuck in the trees, illustrating a harsh reality, but people still refused to believe anything like that was possible. People had trouble comprehending the reality of bodies trapped in trees, but the story is 100 percent true. The photographs showing tractor-trailers and train railcars in trees were more believable. Just imagine someone being swept away by floodwaters and grasping for anything within reach to survive. If you realize your property is flooding and you're trapped, you'd quickly consider climbing a tree to escape the rising, rushing water. There are videos where people sought refuge on the roofs of their homes, only to be swept away in the deadly floodwaters. Desperate to survive, individuals punched holes through their roofs to escape drowning. No matter how uncomfortable or disheartening these stories may be, they are true, and the voices of the victims will be heard. One family in Swannanoa, North Carolina, barely survived when fast-rising floodwaters reached their knees, forcing them to seek shelter in the attic. Although they escaped through the window to their roof, they had to leave their pets behind in the attic. Amazingly, a woman showed up with a kayak and rescued some of their pets from the attic. Soon, more neighbors appeared to rescue the family one by one from the roof.[xxi]

Humans weren't the only collateral damage from Hurricane Helene's wrath and destruction. Livestock, horses, pets, and wild animals were all unexpected victims of the storm. Consider local farmers who relied on their dairy cows to produce a profit and pay their bills. We have seen pictures of horses, cows, donkeys, and other livestock swimming in lakes and rivers, but flooding from Hurricane Helene was far from being anything close to a leisurely swim. Neither humans nor animals could survive the powerful floodwaters as they careened through farmland, neighborhoods, and roadways.

Hurricane Helene impacted agriculture across multiple counties, and farmers reported losing dozens of cattle and significant land to the floods. Farmers affected by Hurricane Helene suffered losses in many ways. They suffered from injured or dead livestock. They suffered the loss of property, including fencing and farm equipment. The flooding also washed away bales of hay and other farm paraphernalia.[xxii]

How prepared were you for Hurricane Helene?

"My family didn't prepare for the hurricane because we've lived in this area my entire life, and the worst a tropical storm hit us with was minor flooding."

Tell me what you were doing when the storm hit.

"I was at work and got the emergency alert that the dam was about to fail and to evacuate the affected areas, and then phone towers and Internet service went down. I started to panic a little because my child was with my in-laws in Franklin, North Carolina, which is about half an hour from where we work. My husband and I both work at the casino, so we met up, and he told me he was going to leave to get her and come back to take us home."

How concerned were you that the storm delayed him?

"After an hour and a half, he still hadn't shown back up, so I got worried. Had a full-on panic attack, imagining the worst. Then he pulled up and explained that he had to wait on a coworker to come back because her house was being evacuated, and she got a room at the hotel in the casino."

How was your daughter and your neighbors?

"Thankfully, we got our daughter home safe. The farm right down the road from our house got flooded pretty badly and lost about $50k in plant damage alone, but they seem to be recovering fairly well from it. The grocery stores were insane at first. Ingles in Bryson is the biggest grocery store we have, and their distribution center got wrecked, so shelves were bare, and they were cash-only for like a week. So far, in Bryson, it seems things have definitely calmed down. I work housekeeping in the casino, and we're still housing some workers who lost their homes as well as volunteers going out to Asheville every day."

How did you feel about people's reactions to the storm?

"Things that made me angry were outsiders' reactions to it, saying that we should've prepared more, conspiracy theorists not giving us time to recover before saying the government manipulated the storm to wipe out Asheville, people saying we deserved it and it was God's punishment for the south being racist, etc. It felt like not a lot of people on the outside seemed to care that human beings were affected by a devastating storm."

Did you experience anything positive from the storm?

"I have friends in a Discord server that would check up on me and were worried sick because they knew the area I was in, but since [communication] towers were down, I couldn't get a hold of them. The positives would be seeing how much our communities really care about each other. It was relieving to see a break in all the political banter and to see people just treating each other like humans during a stressful election year."

Some people moved away after the storm. Have you considered going anywhere else?

"As far as staying, Bryson City is my home. Even if I could afford to move, I'd probably still stay close enough to the area because I love it here."

Do you have anything else you'd like to add?

"I didn't realize the devastation in Asheville until the next day because of the towers and Internet being down. I also didn't know if my mom was okay for three days because I couldn't get a hold of her, but she was fine, just stuck at her house without service. Yeah, I'm very thankful that my family and everyone close to me are okay.

Seeing the destruction of Asheville and hearing stories of everyone else still breaks my

heart."

Tuckasegee River - Bryson City, North Carolina

When watching television and seeing how people live in Third World Countries, many of us feel empathetic about their situation, but we cannot truly understand their plight. However, after experiencing Helene's nightmarish scenario, we now comprehend what existence without electricity or water truly means. Initially, we were informed that it could be months before potable water would be available. However, volunteers from all over the country traveled to Western North Carolina to assist in the recovery efforts. Twenty-six days after the storm hit, volunteers are still working around the clock to restore utilities to everyone.

Additionally, it was inevitable that traffic accidents would become a daily occurrence without working stoplights. Since stoplights didn't function without power, most people tried to follow the rule of a four-way stop, but accidents continued to occur. No one is sure whether it was because some people didn't know how to proceed through a non-functioning light or whether they chose to ignore the rule. "Sometimes, a traffic light is or appears to be fully blacked out when you approach. In this case, treat the intersection as a four-way stop…Make sure that the other cars have come to a full stop before proceeding into the intersection."[xxiii]

To my chagrin, our apartment complex was without potable water for 20 days, so my husband and I considered relocating from Asheville. Our apartment complex responded quickly and agreed to open the swimming pool, allowing tenants to collect chlorinated water from the pool for use in flushing toilets. After allowing us to skip our rent payment for October, they allowed us to break our lease without any penalties or fees if necessary. We were shocked by their willingness to let us leave without asking questions, given the situation. My husband was prepared to leave Asheville, but I wasn't. I've been living here since 2015; I consider Western North Carolina my home and have no desire to leave.

On the other hand, I heard stories from other friends and coworkers who said their apartment management was sending them reminders the day after Hurricane Helene came through, kindly reminding them that their rent was due as usual and warning them that penalties would be incurred if payments were late. No one could believe our apartment allowed us to skip a rent payment, and I still find it shocking. Additionally, I have learned that our lease guarantees that the apartment complex will provide tenants with potable water. Therefore, by law, our apartment could not charge us rent without risking a lawsuit. If this ever happens again, I will strongly suggest that my friends and coworkers confirm their lease agreements to see if the same issues apply to them.

Many stories on social media clouded the truth and misled unsuspecting people about the disastrous situation. In October, North Carolina government officials declared 25 of the State's 100 counties disaster areas, causing historical flooding and killing at least 115 people. The following are the **five most misleading claims** about Hurricane Helene relief efforts:

1. "Chimney Rock residents were told their land was being seized by the federal government. (This claim was false, however, due to the altered topography in Chimney Rock; people who lost homes or buildings won't be able to rebuild them where they last stood.)

2. Joe Biden told the people of North Carolina they had no more supplies. (North Carolina's Lt. Governor made this claim in an Oct. 2 post and has been unable to substantiate the claim.)

3. North Carolina's House Speaker was stopping out-of-state helicopters from flying into damaged areas. (The person who made this claim was not involved in the helicopter matter and did not know the situation.)

4. One thousand troops in North Carolina are sitting around because the governor hasn't distributed the mission orders required for troops to be deployed. (The governor asked the President on Sept. 30 to make all necessary federal resources available to respond to the catastrophic storm. A letter was written to the U.S. Defense Secretary giving consent allowing the North Carolina Army National Guard to lead response efforts in North Carolina."[xxiv]

Tunnel Road - Asheville, North Carolina

Tunnel Road - Asheville, North Carolina

Tunnel Road - Asheville, North Carolina

Tunnel Road - Asheville, North Carolina

CHAPTER SEVEN

The Aftermath

"Nobody expected this. It wasn't just the hurricane; it was all the rainwater two days before."

CHAPTER SEVEN: The Aftermath

DAY 1 – SEPTEMBER 27, 2024

Rivers throughout Western North Carolina swallowed communities, leaving behind mud and debris, creating a nightmarish scene of absolute destruction. The French Broad River in Fletcher crested at 30.31 feet today. The Swannanoa River at Biltmore crested at 26.1 feet, more than five feet above what it did at its maximum in the 1916 flood.[xxv] On Patton Avenue in Asheville, a vehicle was driving along when several trees fell onto the roof of the car. The driver's condition is unknown.

DAY 2 – SEPTEMBER 28, 2024

"Although Helene is now a post-tropical cyclone, near the Kentucky-Indiana border, widespread significant river flooding continues across the southern Appalachians. Maximum sustained winds are still near 25 mph with even higher gusts…at least 45 people have lost their lives across five states as millions remain without power following Hurricane Helene's destructive path."[xxvi]

DAY 3 – SEPTEMBER 29, 2024

As of today, 95 people have died across six states: South Carolina, Georgia, Florida, North Carolina, Virginia, and Tennessee. In North Carolina, 36 deaths have been confirmed by county and state officials. There are 25 dead in South Carolina, including two firefighters in Saluda County. In Georgia, at least 17 people have died, two of them killed by a tornado in Alamo. In Florida, of the 11 deceased, several drowned in Pinellas County. Additionally, two people have died in Virginia, and four others have died in Tennessee.[xxvii]

Officials in Buncombe County, North Carolina, received about 600 missing person reports through an online form. At least 30 people are known to have died in Buncombe County. Officials encouraged people to remain hopeful and reiterated that the lack of communication would probably explain the filing of so many missing persons reports. Many of the missing would be found once communications were restored.

The US Department of Transportation reported that 300 roads in North Carolina and 150 roadways in South Carolina were closed due to flooding and unsafe conditions. The numerous road closures limited the speed and ability of anyone to deliver much-needed water supplies to communities in need. According to PowerOutage.us, millions of residents and businesses in the Southeastern United States were without power. "About 2.1 million power customers are in the dark in South Carolina, North Carolina, Georgia, Florida, and Virginia". However, Duke Energy's utility operations in South Carolina believed that most customers would have their power restored by Friday.[xxviii]

On Sunday, the federal government declared a public health emergency in North Carolina. They sent 200 people to the state to assess the impact on hospitals, nursing homes, and other care facilities. President Joe Biden approved federal disaster declarations in Florida, Georgia, Alabama, North Carolina, Tennessee, and Virginia. In addition, Helene had already dumped 12 to 14 inches of rain in South Carolina, 12 to 16 inches in Florida, and 12 to 14 inches in Georgia. The National Weather Service predicted additional rainfall throughout the weekend across the southern parts of the Appalachian region.[xxix]

Attorney General Josh Stein received numerous complaints of price gouging in the aftermath of Hurricane Helene. "The Department of Justice has received 64 complaints alleging price gouging in Western North Carolina. Most complaints are about hotel rates, grocery prices, and fuel prices…The Attorney General's Office is investigating these complaints and has already sent three civil investigative demands to learn more about some of these concerns."[xxx]

"Chimney Rock – a tiny tourist town of 140 people just east of Asheville – was reduced to nothing more than mounds of brown sludge and washed-away roadways that hampered rescue efforts…It was unclear how many were dead in the small town. But in Buncombe County, which neighbors Rutherford County, encompassing Chimney Rock, at least 40 perished as of Monday night."[xxxi]

DAY 5 – OCTOBER 1, 2024

As of October 1, 2024, Hurricane Helene has killed at least 60 people. All the roads in the western part of North Carolina were closed. "People across Western North Carolina 'chain-sawed' their way to loved ones and drove for hours Saturday on dwindling gas tanks in search of food and power, in what one resident described as a 'mini-apocalypse' after Hurricane Helene."[xxxii]

DAY 6 – OCTOBER 2, 2024

President Biden toured areas in Western North Carolina. "The North Carolina Department of Justice received more than 100 price gouging complaints during and after Hurricane Helene, a spokesperson reported Wednesday. Josh Stein said, 'Unfortunately, there are some bad actors who are out there trying to take advantage of this crisis to make an extra buck off people's desperation. Charging too much for any needed good or service during an emergency is against the law in North Carolina…Residents wrote on Facebook and through a state tip line that some gas stations in Western North Carolina were charging as much as $10 per gallon in the storm's wake."[xxxiii]

As of today, preliminary reports show that Hurricane Helene is the fifth-deadliest hurricane to strike the United States. According to the National Hurricane Center, the following is a list of the Top Ten Deadliest Hurricanes:

1. Katrina, 2005: 1,392 deaths
2. Audrey, 1957: 416 deaths
3. Camille, 1969: 256 deaths
4. Sandy, 2012: 219 deaths
5. Helene (preliminary), 2024: 214 deaths
6. Diane, 1955: 184 deaths
7. Ian, 2022: 156 deaths
8. Agnes, 1972: 122 deaths
9. Harvey, 2017: 103 deaths
10. Hazel, 1954: 95 deaths[xxxiv]

DAY 7 – OCTOBER 3, 2024

"More than 200 people have died due to Hurricane Helene. In North Carolina, 115 people have died. In addition, South Carolina has reported 41 fatalities, Georgia 33, Florida 19, Tennessee 11, and Virginia 2 for a total of 214. Hundreds are still missing in Western North Carolina."[xxxv]

DAY 11 – OCTOBER 7, 2024

Following Hurricane Helene's departure, 230 people have lost their lives, and communities suffered billions of dollars of damage across the Southeast. U.S. Homeland Security Secretary reported that the Federal Emergency Management Agency (FEMA) had sufficient disaster relief following Hurricane Helene, but a forthcoming funding shortage was anticipated. It was believed that Congress may need to approve additional funding once the dust cleared and proper assessments had been made. FEMA claimed that federal assistance provided to survivors had surpassed $137 million. The U.S. Department of Transportation's Federal Highway Administration (FHWA) freed up $100 million in Emergency Relief funds for the North Carolina Department of Transportation for immediate emergency work.

In comparison, Hurricane Katrina, which tore through Florida and the Deep South in August 2005, is one of the deadliest and costliest natural disasters in the United States. There were about 2,000 fatalities and an estimated $125 billion in damage. According to the Library of Congress's Congressional Research Service, $121.7 billion in hurricane relief was allocated for disaster relief following Katrina, as well as the less destructive Hurricanes Rita (September 2005), Wilma (October 2005, Gustav (August 2008), and Ike (September 2008).[xxxvi]

DAY 14 – OCTOBER 10, 2024

In Asheville, North Carolina, contractors were working diligently to reconnect the main 36-inch water line, providing the community with the hope that repairs were occurring much faster than expected. It was a significant accomplishment for more than 70% of Buncombe County and the City of Asheville, which remained without water resources.[xxxvii]

DAY 15 – OCTOBER 11, 2024

The water supply in Black Mountain is "not drinkable even if boiled...we're still in the first stage of the restoration process...A town curfew, from 7 p.m. – 6 a.m., remains in effect."[xxxviii]

"Areas in and around Mitchell County received two feet of rainfall over 24 hours.

Cars, pickup trucks, and school buses got caught up in the flood, their wreckage mired in the mud. Micaville became the gateway to devastation and lost all contact with the outside world during the days that followed. Businesses on Locust Street in downtown Spruce Pine were flooded by the swollen North Toe River. Mass casualties from back-to-back Category 4 hurricanes in the South put a strain on the national supply of intravenous fluids to hospitals and dialysis centers. Still, Helene also disrupted the production of IV products at the Baxter Healthcare plant in North Cove, north of Marion, that produces a substantial portion of those products for the nation."[xxxix]

DAY 16 – OCTOBER 12, 2024

Today was the first day that Swannanoa started to get nonpotable water. Amazingly, this was possible, so soon after the storm, but potable water would take much longer.

DAY 18 – OCTOBER 14, 2024

"North Fork started putting 12 million gallons of raw water into the system, and residents in downtown, north, and south started to get nonpotable water gurgling in their pipes. Residents are put on a boil notice, and some residents start to shower and do laundry again."[xl]

DAY 19 – OCTOBER 15, 2024

Nonpotable water has reached West Asheville. "A significant portion of the city's water system has seen the return of nonpotable water after weeks without running drinkable water; however, it remains out of reach as the city began an in-lake treatment process."[xli]

"Hurricane Helene flooded our town of Marshall, NC, leaving behind over 2 feet of toxic muck inside all the buildings and filling all the streets. Our community has come together in a grassroots effort to clean up the town. The job requires the use of heavy equipment, including excavators, skid steers, dump trucks, and tractors. Community members have also brought their equipment to assist with the work. So far, over 1000 tons of construction debris and even more mud have been hauled off, with much work still to be completed. The flood through our town was devastating. The flood water rose to 27 feet! That is 3 feet above the previous record flood of 1916. As we walked through the streets, people were in a state of total despair, unsure of how to proceed. The equipment operators have been working for two weeks in the mud, dust, and debris of unknown sources and chemical compositions."[xlii]

DAY 22 – OCTOBER 18, 2024

"We cleaned out a flooded house that was a total loss. The lady was elderly and precious, sweet and heartbroken over her home and all she had been through. On top of her loss of house and home, she lost her brother. He lived across the street from her. His home was ripped in half by the river, and he was stuck in a tree for many hours before he washed away. She lost everything and must bury her brother. I am wondering if funerals are covered somehow or if this is also a financial burden for families on top of everything else. If there is no aid for funerals, is there any legit way to help?"[xliii]

DAY 25 – OCTOBER 21, 2024

Ninety-five people are confirmed dead, along with 26 people who are still missing in North Carolina.[xliv] President Trump visited Swannanoa, North Carolina, today.

After I missed a week of work, I was relieved to see that some employers were able to reopen their doors. Without income, people were worried about the bills that continued to come in. A coworker said the following: "I've asked for a day off from work because I feel like I didn't get a moment to get over the trauma of the storm. I feel like I wasn't allowed to breathe, and I wanted to spend the day cleaning stuff." I nodded in agreement because all I wanted to do was keep myself busy. I volunteered at the Beaverdam Community Center to help organize clothing and food donations from the community. It was to be productive and able to help others, which took my mind off my problems. No matter how bad you think you have it, someone else always has it worse. We received numerous donations, which took a few days to organize for ease of searching and access by community members.

I got my Internet and cell phone coverage back about five days after the storm, but it was intermittent and unreliable. If I sat outside, I had a better chance of keeping a connection, but I soon discovered that seeing all the videos of destruction was depressing and harmful to my mental health. It was like I couldn't look away, but the more I watched, the sadder I got. One story chilled me to the core because it involved 11 family members dying in a massive mudslide. The son watched his parents get swept away in the torrent of mud, and there was absolutely nothing he could do to save them.

In another story, a couple tried to save their child by tying the child to a tree. It didn't help him survive. Also, a rescue team found a man buried up to his neck in the mud, and when rescuers tried to help him, he told them to leave him alone. They asked him where his family was, and he said they were buried underneath him. A family of three got stuck on a flooded road. Rescuers were able to pull the mother to safety, but her husband and child perished.

I want to ask my readers, "What's the longest you've been without water or electricity?" Twenty-six days after Hurricane Helene hit North Carolina, people were still without water and electricity. It was nine days before I got to take a shower at a friend's house. In the meantime, I had to boil bottled water to clean the most sensitive areas of my body. To wash my hair, I used room-temperature water bottles, but I felt guilty wasting our potable water on my hair. Luckily, I was without power for only three days. It was the twenty days without water that frustrated me the most. Even with the water, we're still under a boil advisory and must continue to use bottled water for drinking and brushing our teeth. We were advised to add bleach to water when washing our dirty dishes. I've made sure to remove my cup from the bathroom sink so that I don't accidentally drink sink water in the middle of the night or first thing in the morning when I take my medication.

We also must remember to share our bottled water with our pets to keep them safe. You never realize how essential water is to everyday living. Taking the availability of water for granted, I will do my best to conserve this precious resource. I don't think I'll ever forget what it felt like not knowing when or where we'd get more water.

While running errands the other day before work, I used my GPS to take the backroads. I hadn't even thought about road closures, but once I started following the voice-directed instructions, I saw a significant amount of trash and debris on the sides of the roads and beside the riverbank. I soon realized that my GPS was leading me to the Biltmore Village area, which was closed to the public. I was worried that with the massive amounts of storm debris blocking the roads, I'd have to turn around and backtrack, but the main roads were open. However, I could see everything the floodwaters left behind in Biltmore Village. It was surreal to see roads blocked off with police officers standing guard. Videos and photographs help paint a picture of what happened in Asheville, but seeing it first-hand is both powerful and overwhelming.

DAY 26 – OCTOBER 22, 2024

"Deaths caused by the hurricane surpassed 300 people, making Helene the second-deadliest hurricane in the U.S. this century. That number was surpassed only by Katrina in 2005, which killed 1,392 people. In North Carolina, officials say 96 people are confirmed dead thus far, with that number expected to rise as rescue crews search for missing persons. The highest number of deaths occurred in Buncombe County, 42 people.

In the days following the storm, the Buncombe County Sheriff's Office initially reported 72 Helene-related deaths. The NCDHHS confirmed a range of causes of death due to Helene's excessive wind and rainfall. The following are the most common causes of death:

- Unknown circumstances: Three
- Drowning: 33
- Landslide: 23
- Wind/tree trauma: Six
- Motor vehicle drownings: Four

- Blunt force injuries: 18
- Motor vehicle crash: Three
- Environmental exposure: One
- Other: Five"[xlv]

DAY 29 – OCTOBER 25, 2024

First Lady Jill Biden visited Asheville to serve meals and praise Hurricane Helene volunteers at the World Central Kitchen.[xlvi]

An Asheville City Council report explained that installing fuse gates in 2020 was the only reason complete annihilation didn't occur in Western North Carolina. The dam held back six billion gallons of water, which, had it been breached, would have caused thousands of deaths.

DAY 30 – OCTOBER 26, 2024

Today is the 30-day anniversary of Hurricane Helene, and time is continuing as though nothing happened. We see heavy traffic on the roads, as usual. Communities are doing their best to find a new normal by providing something fun for the kids for Halloween. And parents are ready for a respite from the stress of the storm. Yesterday, some school systems had a two-hour delay due to mandated road closures. People have started wondering whether students will continue through the summer months to make up for missed days. The situation is reminiscent of the first days of the COVID-19 epidemic, a terrifying time that no one wants to revisit.

DAY 32 – OCTOBER 28, 2024

The stress and frustration of living through trauma finally got to me, so I decided to soak in a hot tub of bath water. Leaving only a night light switched on, I let the water run until it covered my hips and legs. Glancing down at the filled tub, I noticed it getting darker and darker. Grabbing my cell phone, I took a picture of the water with the flash on so I could see. To my horror, I soon realized I was soaking in a tub of muddy water and needed to get out immediately. After I had shared my picture with friends and coworkers, everyone commented, "I can't believe you got into that nasty water." I gently reminded them that I had turned off the lights in hopes of destressing and relaxing, but I still sounded crazy because I probably should have realized that now was not the time to soak.

West Asheville/Leicester, North Carolina

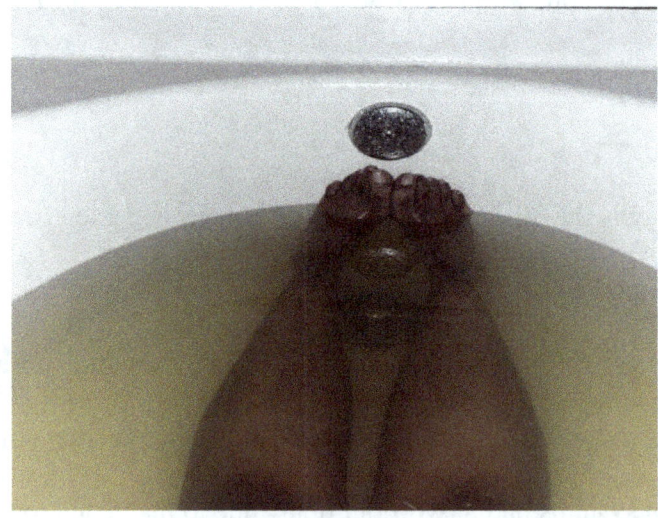

"Entire buildings [along the Swannanoa River] are missing, and train cars are cast across private property, rolled over, and tossed around like they weigh nothing in the 30' torrent of water…We have finalized some data for the impacts on our Asheville structures. 409 has damage in some areas, but other regions are operable. They've been marked yellow. One hundred eighty-two buildings have been marked unsafe to occupy and are designated red. Nine hundred eight units (or buildings you choose) have passed inspection and are marked green, meaning safe to occupy. In Buncombe, they've now detailed their numbers into residential vs commercial. Six hundred one residential structures need major work. Two hundred ninety-four have been destroyed, and two hundred forty-one commercial buildings need major work. One hundred fifty-three have been destroyed. Spectrum [communications] is at 97% restored, with 2900 accounts left unrestored. No timeline to announce on those last accounts."[xlvii]

Swannanoa, North Carolina

DAY 34 – OCTOBER 30, 2024

Today is the first day that the City of Asheville experiments with mixing small amounts of treated water with raw water.

DAY 35 – OCTOBER 31, 2024

Happy Halloween. Everyone is fearful and is praying for access to potable (drinkable) water. The current estimate is mid-December. Although it's raining, we're learning that a light, steady rain can help with turbidity. The first question that comes to mind with this report is how we will celebrate Thanksgiving without potable water.

DAY 36 – NOVEMBER 1, 2024

The day has been somber, something unusual for a Friday, and it's been raining. Different people have posted on social media about their anxiety whenever they see a raindrop. Flashing back to the memories of the horrors of the flood, people are trying to learn how to deal with their new normal. Rain used to be a frivolous nuisance often ignored, but now has become an enemy that can unleash death and destruction if it gets out of control. Friends try to calm one another, suggesting they breathe, count to ten, meditate, or seek the help of a counselor. I found myself thinking about the dead as the rain splattered against my car window. Feeling like I'm living in a dream, I try to focus on driving to work, but as I pass the French Broad River, I can see debris and mud piled on the riverbanks and the side of the road. I'm thankful that they finally removed the minivan destroyed by trees and said a little prayer that no one perished in the vehicle.

After arriving at work, I engaged in conversation with my coworker, and she told me that authorities had found more bodies in some areas. I'm sickened by the thought of the condition of the bodies this late after the storm. Remember that there are friends and families still searching for their loved ones, holding onto the hope of survival when we all know in our hearts that they are gone. There is no hope of anyone being found alive at this juncture. Although everyone understands this truth, no one dares to speak it. We're all holding on to a thin thread that threatens to break if another event comes our way. Now, our lives are filled with unspoken prayers for those we have lost, silent tears flow in our dreams, and the hope that Hurricane Helene is both the first and the last time that we experience an apocalyptic nightmare of destruction.

Later in the day, the City of Asheville announced it had started producing 10 million gallons a day of treated water, about 40% of the needed capacity. They will continue to mix the treated water and raw water (untreated) into the system.

DAY 37 – NOVEMBER 2, 2024

"NC has 39 counties impacted by Helene, over 100 deaths, fourteen hundred landslides, almost a million structures were without power, 163 losses of water and sewer systems, 400 hazardous waste facilities, and 10 million cubic yards of debris. There is an estimated cost of $53.6 billion in damages. Finding help and giving help are still the primary focus for most of the region. Many remain without work, many have rent and mortgage payments due, and many continue to live in shelters and hotels."[xlviii]

DAY 38 – NOVEMBER 3, 2024

Another person anonymously posted on social media the following on November 4, 2024: "I can tell you, again and again, to be gentle with yourself and, if you're like me, it will still be hard to comprehend HOW gentle with yourself you need to be. It's okay to be all things at once, both okay and not. Grateful and grieving. Determined and despairing. The soul of Asheville is strong, but you don't have to be, not all the time. It's okay to collapse. Just don't stay there forever. Hang on. Do whatever you need to do to get yourself through. Grief and love go hand in hand, and it's okay to walk with both. #ashevillestrong #AppalachiaStrong #WNCStrong #survival."[xlix]

DAY 39 – NOVEMBER 4, 2024

Since Hurricane Helene blew through Western North Carolina, nothing has been the same as before. Even the traffic has been worse than usual, which is unusual considering all the damage and loss of property that we've experienced. People have reported "looky-loos," individuals who visit the area to take pictures of the destruction. Additionally, tourists continue to visit Western North Carolina, likely seeking to help us recover economically. Yesterday, I spoke to three people who work at the laundry and shower site provided by Wells Fargo in Candler, North Carolina. One lady was from Alabama, and one man was from Myrtle Beach, South Carolina. They told me they'd been here since Hurricane Helene hit and hadn't seen their families since before the storm.

I keep asking myself, "What kind of people selflessly leave the safety and warmth of their own homes to come and help a bunch of strangers?" I've spoken to people who have come to North Carolina to bring food, water, clothes, propane, generators, money, and more in hopes of helping someone or anyone. When you think that the world is going to Hell in a handbasket, something like this happens and shows you that there are still good people in the world. No matter our political affiliations or religion, we all understand the need for love and support during such a horrific event. Living through and with trauma isn't easy for anyone, and Hurricane Helene has broken the best of us. Fortunately, we've had people to hold us up and support us during our darkest days.

DAY 40 – NOVEMBER 5, 2024

Today is Election Day, and although Helene turned our world upside down, people didn't let it keep them from casting their votes. Voting calculations showed that 127,360 residents of Buncombe County had already voted early. By 10:00 a.m., another 10,000 residents had voted.

DAY 41 – NOVEMBER 6, 2024

"A 1000-year flood means that there is a 1 in 1000 chance (.1%) of happening over 10 years. What this really boils down to is that we have been and will continue to be at risk for flooding, and we must act accordingly. As more stories surface, a trend is arising. A lot of damage to buildings happened because of objects like U-Hauls, cars, semis, train cars, and large tanks thrusting about in the high waters."[1]

DAY 43 – NOVEMBER 8, 2024

The USDA Forest Service estimated damage to more than 187,000 acres of the Nantahala and Pisgah National Forests, roughly 20 percent of the total acreage.

The City of Asheville officials suggested that citizens perform the following actions to protect their home appliances from excessive sediment deposits:

- Flip off the breaker to your water heater.

- Turn off the water to your water heater.

- Turn off the hot water under your sinks.

- Remove the aerator on faucets. *Note*: *Typically, it just unscrews.*

- Turn off the ice maker.

- Turn off the water to your whole-house filter if you have one.

- When water returns, flush your pipes by running water in a bathtub faucet or outdoor faucet for about 15 minutes and flush the toilet(s).

New Leicester Highway - West Asheville, North Carolina

DAY 44 – NOVEMBER 9, 2024

"Forty-four days of thousands of people across the region mobilizing, refusing to give up, and slowly rebuilding are taking some shape. Some severely impacted areas remain in complete disarray, with debris and crumbled buildings untouched. There are clusters of tents and campers in Swannanoa. It's a mixed bag of progress and emotions as part of the city comes alive, while others remain in dire straits. Buncombe County received its first FEMA-supplied manufactured home this past week. As of today, FEMA has approved $225 million to more than 123,000 households in North Carolina. More than 4,450 households are checked into transitional hotels and motels. AVL Watchdog reported that WNC lost 822,000 acres of trees, and 40% of Buncombe County trees were damaged."[li]

DAY 45 – NOVEMBER 10, 2024

"Cleanup is still going on; Helene left behind 3 million cubic yards of debris. Some roads are not usable. Some areas of town are unrecognizable and may never look the same again. I-40 going into Tennessee is still closed as well. The last report stated that there are 101 people dead due to the hurricane, and 10 people are still unaccounted for. This past Thursday, a memorial was held for a Buncombe County student and his grandparents. All three died when the roof of their home collapsed. I cannot begin to tell you how much I cried. I will continue to shed tears for my community and the losses we all feel."[lii]

DAY 48 – NOVEMBER 13, 2024

"Before Helene, almost half of the residents were cost-burdened, meaning they spent more than 30% of their income on housing, something that affects all other aspects of their lives. Until recently, we had the highest rents in the state."[liii]

DAY 49 – NOVEMBER 14, 2024

Today, we remain without potable water, but most other utilities are working again. The piles of debris seem insurmountable, and no one knows how long it will take for repairs to be complete. Thousands of vehicles, damaged buildings, and trees litter our communities. Buncombe County Manager Avril Pender said, "The debris is a 'football field a mile high'…Our landfills cannot handle the amount of debris incurred, so, much like this entire process, we are relying on other communities' assistance."[liv]

DAY 50 – NOVEMBER 15, 2024

Yesterday's bad news: Seven schools tested positive for lead inside their plumbing pipes. Good news: The North Fork treatment system is now capable of delivering potable water to City of Asheville customers, marking the official start of the flushing and testing phase. However, everyone is still under a boil notice until all testing is complete. Early estimates are that we may be able to drink and cook with water on or before November 20th.

DAY 51 – NOVEMBER 16, 2024

"Wow, out of the blue, the city announces that we'll have potable water next week. This comes after weeks of tracking high turbidity levels in the North Fork Reservoir and significant attempts to reduce those levels and/or have the Army Corps of Engineers construct a temporary pre-filter system by early December. I strongly suspect that what has changed is that the city officials have decided to accept much higher levels of manganese in the drinking water than what would normally be acceptable. The pressure for this decision is obvious: getting the city and restaurants open before Thanksgiving."[lv]

DAY 52 – NOVEMBER 17, 2024

Numerous individuals have reported being denied FEMA assistance despite applying for the $750 payment. It blows my mind that people in need during a natural disaster would have a problem, but I must admit that the application questions were tricky, and I wasn't sure I could answer correctly. Thankfully, Pisgah Legal Services, a nonprofit law firm, offered a free help clinic for anyone who received a denial.

Water tests conducted at several schools found significant amounts of lead in their water pipes. However, officials explained that lead will naturally accumulate in any pipes if not used for a month or more.

DAY 53 – NOVEMBER 18, 2024

Officials lifted the systemwide Boil Water Notice in Asheville today. The November 16 and 17 samplings were clear of contaminants. Communities were also encouraged to support local businesses by patronizing their local establishments, if possible.

DAY 54 – NOVEMBER 19, 2024

The City of Asheville agreed to temporarily lift housing restrictions allowing people without housing to reside in an RV or tiny home on wheels for 180 days, with the option to extend the stay if necessary. However, many people are disheartened that a moratorium on evictions and foreclosures never passed, so tenants must continue to pay rent or mortgages on time, even if their homes are destroyed or uninhabitable.

DAY 55 – NOVEMBER 20, 2024

Tonight, a Code Purple warning is in effect, which means that shelter rules will be modified to accommodate emergency temporary housing for the homeless.

DAY 56 – NOVEMBER 21, 2024

Unfortunately, after two months, many impacted areas look as though no one has touched them. It's getting colder, and many people are still living in tents, campers, vans, and cars. WLOS reported that 1,152 students in Buncombe County were without homes.

Strangely, the Red Cross closed six emergency shelters. Today, only 1,000 people are sheltering in hotels and motels.[lvi]

"Northern Buncombe County has a small community called Barnardsville. Many suffered damage, while others lost everything. Homes and vehicles floated downstream. Farm animals and pets are carried away. Cleanup and rebuilding have begun, but there will be months before any semblance of normality returns."[lvii]

Flooding also destroyed the Rainbow Bridge and the surrounding area. Efforts are underway to rebuild the bridge, but pet collars and other memorabilia in remembrance of fur babies were lost in the storm.

Lake Lure and Chimney Rock, North Carolina

<u>Where were you on the day of the storm?</u>

"The day of the storm, I was scheduled to fly out to Colorado to meet a friend. I had to bring my dog to my son's house so he could take care of it, but as I came out of the house to take out the trash, it was pouring rain, and I slipped in the mud and had to go back inside to change my clothes. I then got in my car and headed towards the bridge, but I couldn't reach it because all the trees down, and it was underwater. It was seven o'clock. So, I went up to the gap, and there were four sets of trees down, and half the road had been washed out. I saw trees falling like matchsticks, and that was the craziest thing I had ever seen. One hit the back of my car and broke a taillight, and then a branch fell on my windshield but didn't break it. So, I raced home because I couldn't do it anymore. As it stopped raining, I had to walk up to the gap and go through the four sets of downed trees, and they were big. I was able to get a signal, and it was breaking in and out, but I called my kids and friend to let them know I was okay. Then the cell phone service went out, and then I went down to help others with chainsaws to take the trees off. There was a woman due with her first child that day, so a neighbor had a bulldozer and took trees off the bridge that was still standing and got her to the fire station."

<u>What about your other neighbors?</u>

"I have an 80-year-old friend who lives next to a guy who keeps after her, and they're right at the creek. Six years ago, the bridge was washed away by a storm, so it was reinforced with concrete. The water rose quickly, and he was okay, but he tried to get over to her, but the water was flowing like 60 mph with trees and everything. His house has two stories, and the water got up to the second story, and the water was slapping against his door. The water was getting into her house, and she was sitting there with her dog, praying to God, saying she's ready to go, but not this way. She could feel her house vibrating as the trees and stuff were hitting her house, and she was helpless. The concrete bridge saved his house and diverted the water and debris around it. She survived, but all her Angora goats, which were her livelihood, were washed away. As the water receded, there were big logs against her front porch, which was damaged, but it was actually a car that was crunched up that was protecting everything. We think it was God who was protecting that. She's still unable to live in the house, and they condemned it. Another elderly couple who owned a pottery business were saved by another house that had been solidly built, but a tree hit it and knocked it off its foundation. That house blocked and protected their home, but there was still a lot of damage, so they left and moved to Tennessee, and they're not coming back."

<u>Where is your 80-year-old friend living now?</u>

"She's living with her friend next door, but that's tough. They had a flood surveyor come, and he said that anything below the second floor has to be redone, but he moved up to the second story. She's still homeless, and she had a friend who had taken two of her goats years ago and will give them back to her. There are all kinds of river rocks surrounding her house, and the French Broad River and the Flat Rock Creek converge there."

<u>Have you ever seen anything like this before?</u>

"No, I've lived in Barnardsville for five years, but I came from New York and never saw any storms like this. I was in the military and moved out when I was 19. We had flooding, like calm water, but it wasn't anything like this. This water was angry and raging. But I lived in Florida for 20 years and have seen hurricanes, but this was the worst because of the trees, and when you're on the side of the mountain, there is only one way for water to go. Reems Creek had the dam, and it overflowed, and they had to release that, but they waited too long. Nobody expected this. It wasn't just the hurricane; it was all the rainwater two days before. That's why all the trees were falling over. The roots couldn't sustain the trees because the ground was too saturated."

<u>What else have you seen since the storm?</u>

"I did some work out in Pensacola, North Carolina, for Samaritan's Purse and worked for a church, and that's Cane Creek out there. It's usually 100 feet wide, and after the storm, it expanded to 1000 feet. They lost people there and found people in trees. I get pissed off when people on the west side say it's not really that bad. They just took the crumbled cars out last week. Can you imagine falling into that water and finding yourself in one piece, let alone alive?

I also heard a story about a couple renting an Airbnb out in Pensacola, near Cane Creek. There was water all around the house, and they were panicking. They didn't have any provisions and didn't know who to call. No food, and the power is out. The fire department came days later and were able to cross [Cane Creek], and the family and their kids were seeing bodies lying in the field, and it was absolutely horrible. They had cadaver dogs, and there were stacks of mud and everything else. One guy told me that the best way to find someone who is missing is by their shoe. They'll find something in their shoe. That's the only way they know.

Further out in Pensacola, they had mudslides. One house got knocked halfway over the mountain with a 20-foot drop below. She was in the house and heard this god-awful rumble. And she was in the kitchen, and the kitchen table kind of fell and saved her, and she was trapped. Oh, I also heard something else, but I'm not sure if it's true. I heard that in Pensacola, there was a van with people in it trying to cross the bridge, and a wave swept them away."

Do you have any advice for people facing similar natural disasters?

"Take yourselves and go to higher ground and don't wait to the last second. The storm last night gave us an inch and a half of rain. I don't know if we'll ever get used to the PTSD from all this. You can have storms all over. For the homes that were wiped away, the government isn't going to allow those homes to be rebuilt there because it's in a flood zone now. FEMA only gave one lady with the house that was moved off the foundation money to rebuild a well and septic tank, and she can't get help with anything else. Who would have thought this? I heard that only 30% of people had flood insurance, and the rest didn't.

I didn't have power for 15 days and had the creek for the toilet, like old times. But you should have a portable radio to know what's going on. I was without power on the east side of the mountain, and there was no cell phone service. When people contacted me to ask if I was okay, I asked why because I didn't know what was going on. With the mountains, you've got to have a signal, so if you're on the wrong side of the mountain, it's tough. It took me a couple of days to even get out."

Were there any positives from this experience?

"The good thing was that everyone, all the neighbors, were checking up on everyone. People checked on me. The mountain folk were going door to door to check on people they didn't even know. Mountain folk didn't hesitate to get it done."

What is the future of tourism in your area?

"A couple of Trails, the Big Ivy [Coleman Boundary] near Barnardsville, is just gone. One bridge, part of the road is gone, and they're not going to rebuild it. 30 feet of trees are blocking the trail. Six-ton boulders were moved; I don't know where they came from. They're doing a really good job of cleaning it up, Barnardsville. Big trucks are moving all this stuff. They repaved the road that was all torn out. People came out with four-wheelers going up the mountain to lots of isolated areas. I didn't see any deaths out there. If you go to Dillingham Road off 197 in Barnardsville, you can see the creek, and they've cleaned most of it up, but see homes and cars twisted. I saw an iron I-beam twisted and bent around a tree."

<u>How are you handling everything? Are you still volunteering?</u>

"I had to go to Knoxville at some point because I couldn't take it anymore. I'd been volunteering with Samaritan's Purse. They're a Christian organization out of The Cove, Billy Graham's place. You can work there for a day, but normally, people go with a cot and the clothes on their back, and Samaritan's Purse provides food and a place to put your cot. It's a very organized situation, and they'll have a list of certain houses to work on. There was one in Pensacola that had about a foot of mud, and 20 or 30 of us were there shoveling the mud out. We had to take all the drywall off and treat it, and then a different team would put it back up. It's physical help, but not financial assistance. People can't afford to do the whole house, especially when insurance won't pay for it. They are completely hands-on. A lot of different Christian associations have helped tremendously. We've gotten so much help from people all over the country, even people driving down from Alaska."

DAY 61 – NOVEMBER 26, 2024

On my way to work today, I began to think about all the people without homes who are now living in tent cities due to Hurricane Helene. It's raining today and 55

119

degrees, but I would imagine that living in a tent for days and days, the temperature doesn't matter either way, because living in a tent is far from living in a house. We here in Asheville have been blessed because the cavalry arrived rather quickly and got us up and going. Now we have water, but other cities are waiting for relief.

Approximately 100,000 people reside in Asheville, but in my opinion, the influx of money and tourists is the primary reason Asheville received so much assistance so quickly. Having a larger population increases the chances of a breakout of diseases like cholera, but we were already experiencing gastrointestinal illnesses from E. coli and listeria. I do continue to worry about a repeat of the flooding. I don't know how people are managing to make it. People and organizations continue to donate money, but there will never be enough resources to make us right again. Additionally, everyone is in the giving mode right now, but what about months later? Officials have warned us that there will come a day when Hurricane Helene is old news, and we'll fall by the wayside, being forgotten and replaced by the next disaster.

DAY 63 – NOVEMBER 28, 2024

Today is Thanksgiving. We survivors are thankful for the lives that we still have. There are various shelters set up to offer hot meals, food, water, and laundry facilities. Many people are preparing for the cold weather that is expected to arrive in our area over the next week. Tonight, I stood in line at Ace Hardware for a couple of hours to get two 20-gallon tanks of propane. In addition to everything else, now we're all worrying about people freezing to death in tents. My apartment sent emails reminding us to drip our water, turn our heat up to at least 65 degrees, and open all the cabinets underneath the sinks. Honestly, a busted water pipe is the least of our worries right now.

A billboard off Patton Avenue read, "Healing happens gradually. Keep going. Keep loving." At this point, that's the only option we have. Either we keep going or quit and hide in a hole somewhere. Sadly, the last of the care stations inside the city is shutting down after providing the community with 3.9 million bottles of water, 22,400-gallon jugs of potable water, 257,000 gallons of nonpotable water, 250,000 MREs, and 2,900 blankets.

Pensacola, a small town in Yancey County, North Carolina, with approximately 500 residents, had most of its homes washed away by the combined forces of Cattail Creek and Cane River. The water swept away Pensacola Road, the only road connecting the community to the outside world.[lviii]

"NOAA data revealed last month that Helene's reach extended into the upper atmosphere, where the hurricane generated shockwaves (also called gravity waves) up in the atmosphere. According to a NOAA release, preliminary data suggest that Hurricane Helene is the deadliest hurricane in the continental U.S. since Hurricane Katrina. Helene directly caused more than 150 deaths, most of which were in the Carolinas."[lix]

Each day, I find it challenging to write about Hurricane Helene and its impact on my home in the mountains. I've seen videos of Fairview, Marshall, Black Mountain, and Swannanoa, and I am still in shock over the absolute destruction of these communities. However, more shocking to me is the realization that we're more than two months past the storm, and these towns still look like they did the day after the storm. Yes, I see that FEMA has been around the area, but it doesn't seem like they're staying for the long term. I read yesterday that the list of care centers distributing water and supplies has been reduced from around ten to only four locations. I ask myself, "Why on earth would these places be closing when the worst of the winter is just starting this week? What about the people without housing or living in tents on their properties?" There are many questions but few answers.

People outside the affected areas are still trying to determine what is true and what is untrue. The anger has reached a fever pitch among people who believe the untruth that the government has done absolutely nothing. However, those of us who have received some assistance still question why our officials haven't done more for the suffering communities and people who are homeless. Photos and videos are accessible everywhere, but people continue to ask me whether I've visited the worst areas. Truth be told, I'm scared to see the destruction and absolute horror, only to realize that there's absolutely nothing I can do to numb the pain or fix the problem. Additionally, I'm dealing with my own depression and emotional state from the trauma, and know that visiting the destruction would not be good for my mental health.

Volunteering is needed, and some people are stronger both mentally and physically than I am. As a suicide survivor, I know that it doesn't take much to push myself over the edge and into the abyss of hopelessness. Friends and acquaintances have reminded me to take care of myself first and not to push myself too hard when trying to report what is happening after the storm. My empathy leads me down the road of sadness, and sometimes, I feel like I've lost my way. So, please forgive me if I'm unable to personally visit all the cities and towns that have been demolished or destroyed.

Through all the noise and reporting, one subject keeps resurfacing, and it's something that I've tried to avoid discussing, but I can't. Why isn't the government doing more for the people of North Carolina? How come there aren't military forces here to help rebuild or clean up downtown Asheville or other towns? These questions keep resurfacing throughout the locals, but I have no answers. All I do know is that I am highly disappointed in the federal government's response to the storm. Yes, people have volunteered their time to help us. Yes, FEMA has been here. Yes, some of us received money and hotel vouchers from FEMA. Yes, we've received clothing, water, and supplies needed. But we continue to have an extreme need for food, shelter, housing, and clean-up assistance.

And don't even get me started talking about these apartments and landlords trying to evict people who don't have homes, clothing, or jobs. I've personally been helping a friend with their rent payments as much as possible. Other people have opened their homes to friends and strangers to keep people from freezing to death or starving. I'm thankful that the City of Asheville lifted the ban on allowing RVs to be placed on properties around the city. I'm grateful for this change, but it's still not enough.

DAY 72 – DECEMBER 7, 2024

Governor Roy Cooper announced that President Biden approved funds for the federal government to cover 90% of Public Assistance, Hazard Mitigation, and Other Needs Assistance after Hurricane Helene.

DAY 74 – DECEMBER 9, 2024

Traffic in the Asheville area is notorious on a good day, so today, I trusted my GPS to get me home via the best route. Surprisingly, it guided me from Hendersonville

Road to the Blue Ridge Parkway. Since Helene, I had not ventured onto the parkway because it had been closed for a long time due to downed trees. I'm not sure what I was expecting, but what I saw was not it. As soon as I turned onto the parkway, I was shocked to see the number of trees down every few feet. It wasn't just old trees, healthy trees, pine trees, and more. What surprised me most was seeing how many trees had been uprooted by the storm. As I continued to drive, I wondered about my safety, seeing trees that had been knocked down or were being held up by other trees or their roots. I made a mental note that I would never dare to drive on the parkway during a heavy rain or windstorm. I was overcome by sadness because I know how vital the parkway is to our tourism economy. Western North Carolina is a thriving hub of tourism. Sometimes, I feel we may never recover from the storm. At times, I had difficulty focusing on the road in front of me as I stared with my mouth wide open at the number of trees destroyed by Helene. I could barely breathe as I realized how the destruction would affect both our wildlife and our economy.

I tried to imagine how the trees would look once the leaves were back out in the springtime. In my mind, I could envision bald spots or open areas that would never fill in with lush vegetation because of the missing trees. It's been two months since Hurricane Helene hit North Carolina, and trees and brush still litter the Parkway, making it difficult to travel. However, my best guess is that the regularly heavy traffic flow made it mission-critical to reopen the parkway. Once I finally exited the parkway, I decided to avoid it for a few months because I couldn't handle seeing the level of devastation due to my anxiety.

DAY 84 – DECEMBER 19, 2024

Christmas is just around the corner, and everything still looks the same about three months later. As the cold temperatures take hold, hundreds of people continue to live in campers and tents.

DAY 67 – JANUARY 2, 2025

Governor Josh Stein signed his first executive order to bring more temporary housing units (travel trailers) to Western North Carolina. At the same time, the state's senators have requested that the current administration arrange for additional housing in the region. The number of homes damaged in Western North Carolina by the storm is estimated between 121,000 and 132,000.[lx]

DAY 71 – JANUARY 6, 2025

The North Carolina Department of Health and Human Services released a list of 104 people who perished in North Carolina because of Hurricane Helene. Out of respect for these families, I will not list any victim names in this book.

DAY 77 – JANUARY 12, 2025

North Carolina authorities designated 27 counties under a major disaster declaration. Sadly, many homes were uninsured. The North Carolina Governor's office estimated that more than 70,000 homes were damaged.

DAY 80 – JANUARY 15, 2025

"Nonprofit BeLoved Asheville has purchased a roughly 8-acre parcel in Swannanoa with plans to build a new 'village' of deeply affordable homes, replicating ongoing work at its East Asheville property where 12 tiny homes are awaiting final steps."[lxi]

DAY 86 – JANUARY 21, 2025

The following homes in Western North Carolina counties were affected by storm damage: destroyed homes - Buncombe 340, Henderson 89, McDowell 92, Yancey 100, Madison 11+, major damage - Buncombe 640, Henderson 354, McDowell 128, Yancey 166, Madison 56, and homes requiring habitability repairs - Buncombe 8,920, Henderson 3,988, McDowell 1,442, Yancey 1,767. Madison 302.

DAY 89 – JANUARY 24, 2025

President Donald J. Trump visited Asheville, North Carolina, today. This was his third visit to Western North Carolina since Hurricane Helene.

DAY 126 – JANUARY 30, 2025

"The North Carolina Medical Examiner's Office listed an additional Hurricane Helene-related fatality in Buncombe County, stemming from the discovery of the person's body on Dec. 20, 2024...the total is now 105 storm-related fatalities, with 43 of those recorded in Buncombe, as of Jan. 29, 2025."[lxii]

DAY 139 – FEBRUARY 12, 2025

"The North Carolina Department of Health and Human Services confirmed more deaths related to Hurricane Helene, five months after the storm devastated much of Western North Carolina…The most recent deaths were related to complications from environmental exposure after a home was washed away in the flooding."[lxiii]

DAY 145 – FEBRUARY 18, 2025

"Work has started to clean Buncombe County waterways after Helene left an enormous amount of debris in rivers, creeks, and lakes...removing all types of eligible debris including vegetative, construction and demolition, vehicles, white goods (washers, dryers, refrigerators) and hazardous waste."[lxiv]

Chimney Rock, North Carolina

Broad River flooding Wilma Dykeman Greenway in River Arts District - Asheville, North Carolina

DAY 176 – MARCH 21, 2025

Next week will be six months since Hurricane Helene changed the lives of millions living in seven states. Hurricane Helene is now considered the second-deadliest hurricane since Hurricane Katrina in 2005. As of this date, there are 248 confirmed deaths, 175 of which are directly connected to the storm's wind and flooding. Indirect deaths total 70, caused by medical complications, fires, and electrocutions from downed power lines. The highest number of deaths, 105, occurred in North Carolina.

The high winds reached speeds of over 90 mph in Banner Elk in Watauga County. Yancey County recorded nearly 31 inches of rainfall. The last record of anything close to that amount was set back in 1957.[lxv]

A FIRESTORM

The three wildfires affecting Polk County, North Carolina, are the newest threat in Western North Carolina. Hurricane Helene not only destroyed our beautiful trees, but she also left a perfect fire-starter across our land. "The Black Cove, Deep Woods, and Fish Hook fires have burned a combined 5,754 acres as of Monday morning. Officials said the fire has crossed into Henderson County in the Big Hungry River area."[lxvi]

DAY 183 – MARCH 28, 2025

There are now ten wildfires burning in North Carolina. Eight wildfires are active in six North Carolina counties. Three of those fires were burning in Polk County in Western North Carolina. Active evacuation orders are in place in some communities.

- Freedom Farm Fire (Leicester) – Buncombe County: 130 acres burned, 100% contained.
- Black Cove Fire (Saluda) – Polk County: 3,410 acres burned, 23% contained.
- Alarka #5 Fire (Bryson City) – Swain County: 1,300 acres burned, 10% contained.
- Rattlesnake Branch Fire (Cruso) – Haywood County: 629 acres burned, 5% contained.
- Montieth Branch Fire (Sylva) – Jackson County: 50 acres burned, 0% contained.
- Deep Woods Fire (Columbus) – Polk County: 3,797 acres burned, 32% contained.
- Crusoe Island Road Fire (Tabor City) – Columbus County: 343 acres burned, 75% contained.
- Fish Hook Fire (Lake Adger) – Polk County: 199 acres burned, 95% contained.[lxvii]
- Table Rock Fire – Pickens County, SC: Crossed the state line into Transylvania County, NC, on March 27.[lxviii]

- A new fire has been reported in Fairview, has reached approximately three acres, and is approximately 85% contained.
- A three-acre fire reported in Yancey County is 100% contained.
- A structure fire has ignited within the Incinerator Road area in Canton.
- The Kitchen Branch Fire in Jackson County is 94 acres and 90% contained.
- A fire in Madison County near Gunter Town Road and Big Laurel Creek in Marshall is less than one acre and 0% contained.[lxix]
- The Saw Branch Road Fire is a brush fire in Candler that has burned 25 acres and is 40% contained.

DAY 195 – APRIL 9, 2025

Much-needed rain moved into Western North Carolina for a couple of days, allowing firefighters to make significant headway in containing the wildfires.

DAY 202 – APRIL 15, 2025

Authorities in Marion ordered evacuations for residents in McDowell County because of a wildfire [Bee Rock Branch Fire] located south of Wild Acres Road and north of Armstrong Creek Road (off NC 226 and near Little Switzerland). It is estimated to be 75 acres, with 0% containment as of 6 p.m. on Tuesday.[lxx]

DAY 203 – APRIL 16, 2025

In Hayesville, Clay County is dealing with the Webb Creek Fire, which has burned 45 acres and is 75% contained. It is located on Webb Cove Road, between South Carter Cove Road and Old Highway 64 West.[lxxi]

The Bee Rock Branch Fire near Little Switzerland has grown to 175 acres. It began as a 3 to 4-acre fire on April 14th. It is racing uphill, devouring storm debris, and is at 0% containment.

Researching the wildfires across North Carolina opened my eyes to the widespread problem of downed trees and dry conditions, shedding light on the need for a complete book devoted to the wildfires. However, this is not that book, and I have had to resist including additional information so that this book publishes before the first anniversary of Hurricane Helene.

CHAPTER EIGHT

Towns and Waterways

"More than 400 roads are closed in Western North Carolina."

CHAPTER EIGHT: Towns and Waterways

During the height of the storm, more than 400 roads were closed in Western North Carolina. First responders rescued more than 200 people from drowning. The city of Busick in Yancey County recorded 30.78 inches of rain, Spruce Pine had 24.12, and Hendersonville came in third with 21.96 inches of rain. Below is a summary of the most notable damage from Hurricane Helene:

- **Black Mountain**: The neighborhoods in Montreat and Swannanoa were destroyed, with homes on fire and many fatalities.

- **Chimney Rock**: The village of Chimney Rock was decimated, as illustrated in the cover photo.

- **Hot Springs**: This small town has a history of flooding due to its location in the floodplain, which encompasses much of downtown.

- **Marshall**: This town is located on the French Broad River, and the buildings in downtown Marshall have waters reaching the first-floor roof.

- **Asheville**: After suffering from major flooding and landslides, Buncombe County suffered the most fatalities in the state.

- **Marion and Old Fort**: Residents of this McDowell County city suffered from major mudslides, flooding, and destruction. Buck Creek in Marion broke a record of 21.44 feet due to the torrential downpours of Hurricane Helene.[lxxii]

- **Swannanoa**: Amid a horrible situation, small businesses have reopened in this small town. The Swannanoa River's floodwaters proved nature's ferocity.

- **Fairview**: Among the many victims of Helene were a family of 11 who perished in the landslide.

- **Mount Mitchell**: This state park will remain closed for several months while necessary repairs are made to the Blue Ridge Parkway.

- **Candler**: Suffering from mudslides and flooding, this town was an unfortunate focus of a fake rumor about "2,000 people trapped in a Candler church."[lxxiii]

- **Barnardsville**: "More than 50 homes, including an entire trailer park, were destroyed when Ivy Creek flooded."[lxxiv]

- **Dillsboro**: "Scotts Creek produced more water than the Tuckasegee [River] could add to its already full load and backed up into Back Street."[lxxv]

- **Nantahala and Pisgah National Forests**: "Gale-force winds toppled thousands of acres of trees. The Forest Service estimated the hurricane caused around 117,000 acres of vegetation loss across the two forests."[lxxvi]

- **Lake Lure**: The Rainbow Bridge, part of Lake Lure Flowering Bridge, is a memorial dedicated to lost dogs and other pets, but Helene washed it away when it dropped 22.5 inches of rain on the area.[lxxvii]

- **Brevard**: Normally, Brevard is an hour's drive from Clemson. Following Helene, it now takes four hours because of the washed-out roads from the flooding.

- **Relief**: An unincorporated community in Mitchell County along the banks of the North Toe River was swallowed by a wall of water that carried away neighbors.

- **Green Mountain**: Another community located above the North Toe River had its concrete bridge snapped in half.[lxxviii]

- **Burnsville**: A small town with a population of 1,623 and located near the Tennessee border, U.S. Highway 19 washed out, and the Chestoa Bridge that crosses the Nolichucky River was destroyed.[lxxix]

- **Highlands and Cashiers**: Multiple power poles snapped like twigs, and the town of Highlands was cut off from the outside world due to power outages and loss of communications. In the same boat, the Cashiers community had MREs, water, and other supplies dropped by a Chinook helicopter. Additionally, the "dam in Sapphire led to a partial washout of US64."[lxxx]

- **Waynesville**: Although Helene withheld the worst it had to offer, the town still incurred millions in damage. "Town government was hit across nearly all departments and lost property, vehicles, infrastructure, and park facilities."[lxxxi]

- **Cullowhee**: A community in shock and horror witnessed flooding from the Tuckasegee River: "Homes swallowed by the Tuck [Tuckasegee River] which had jumped out of its banks and onto the farming fields, rising to N.C. 107 in some places."[lxxxii]

- **North Cove and Linville Falls**: These areas were the most devastated regions in McDowell County. North Cove's population of over 2,200 survived rampaging waters which "cascaded down the nearby mountains in Hurricane Helene." The one bridge that connected the community to the outside world was destroyed, so the Catawba River Lodge became an emergency haven for the community.[lxxxiii]

135

- **Hendersonville**: Flooding was so detrimental to this town that an online video shows neighbors standing in chest-deep water and trying to keep their pets afloat. The National Weather Service reported that 16.15 inches fell.

Seventeen designated river basins exist in North Carolina, but only four basins are contained entirely within the state: Cape Fear, Neuse, White Oak, and Tar-Pamlico. Western North Carolina has five major river basins connecting with the Gulf of Mexico: Hiawassee, Little Tennessee, French Broad, Watauga, and New. The remaining twelve river basins flow to the Atlantic Ocean. There are approximately 37,853 miles of river.[lxxxiv]

Western North Carolina has the following rivers within its boundaries:

1. The Davidson River – North Transylvania County, NC

2. Avery's Creek – a small stream found on the Davidson River

3. Courthouse Creek – headwaters of the French Broad River

4. Looking Glass Creek – one-half mile above the Davidson and Looking Glass

5. East Fork of the French Broad – one of four tributaries of the French Broad

6. North Mills River – Northwestern Henderson County and Hendersonville, NC

7. South Mills River – Northern Transylvania and Henderson County

8. West Fork of the French Broad – Haywood County

9. The French Broad River – Transylvania County, NC/Brevard, NC

10. Tuckasegee River – formed by East and West Fork in Dillsboro, NC[lxxxv]

The surge from the ocean during Hurricane Helene caused all the connecting waterways to fill and overflow with raging water. This reaction explains why Western

North Carolina was flooded and destroyed by such a heavy deluge of unrelenting water. In September, multiple factors converged to exacerbate the dire weather conditions and flooding in Western North Carolina.

1. Precursor rain event: Large hurricanes in the Gulf can cause heavy rain to fall further inland when they combine with a cold front. The Asheville region had already received heavy rainfall days before Hurricane Helene.

2. Size of the storm: Larger storms will bring rain to an area earlier and will last longer.

3. Land topography: Mountains force air to rise and cool, causing vapor to condense and additional precipitation to form as it connects with the tropical system. Then, the heavy moisture is squeezed out of the atmosphere and dumped in a short amount of time.[lxxxvi]

<u>Where were you living when Hurricane Helene hit?</u>

"I was living for the summer in a campground in Maggie Valley. We had a Near a beautiful little creek with rather high banks. There was a bridge crossing the creek."

<u>How prepared were you for the storm?</u>

"We had seen it rain for days, and the water never got higher than the creek bank. So, we did not prep at all. I mean, a hurricane in the mountains? I couldn't wrap my head around what was going to happen."

<u>Describe what happened on September 27, 2024.</u>

"We woke up early, and the creek was raging. There were trees in the water pushing against the bridge. It seemed like we had time to gather our belongings and go. We heard a loud pop and looked out the window to find that the bridge was gone, and the creek had become a raging river. Then it came over the bank. The water washed away our neighbors' fence, allowing it to flood the camper. We put the animals in the carrier, and our neighbors carried them through the water to safety. We then went out, and the river was raging by the camper. The camper behind us was turning sideways and hitting ours. When we went out to wade through the water, the ground beneath us was pure silt from the river, and it was tough to walk. We were trying to hold onto each other, but we were broken apart, and the water began making me fall, and the water grabbed me."

Did you think that your life was over at that moment?

"It was a terrifying moment. Suddenly, out of nowhere, a large man grabbed my backpack and pulled me to safety. We were both safe, but all we made it out with was underwear because I had put it in the backpack."

Where have you been living since you lost the camper?

"I am currently living with my mom and trying to replace everything."

Do you have any advice for anyone in a similar situation?

"I'd remind everyone that sometimes warnings are real. Even if it doesn't seem possible."

Can you think of any positives from this situation?

"The most positive thing I can say I found was a) I am alive and b) people coming together in those communities to try and help one another."

Is there anything that makes you angry about what happened here?

"I guess the thing that makes me the angriest is how long people were just stuck with nothing but a mess. I stayed in a hotel that night because we couldn't get out, but the next morning, I went back to Tennessee. My heart broke and still breaks for people who were hit the hardest."

Do you have any comments for the government?

"For the government in general, help was not sent in time. FEMA did its job for the most part, but again, far too late. Many lives were lost. It was devastating."

Highway 70 - Marion, North Carolina

Catawba River – Marion, North Carolina

CHAPTER NINE

The Dark Side

"Most of the repairs and clean-up are being performed by local civilians."

CHAPTER NINE: The Dark Side

The efforts of locals have been the saving grace during this disastrous situation. People expected more assistance from the government, but that has been few and far between. FEMA has given out $750 to multiple families but has denied it to others. A few apartment complexes have extended their leases to their renters, while others have begun filing evacuation orders with the court. One family received a FEMA offer of $300,000 for their destroyed property, but another said they received no offer. FEMA set up a station in Marshall, but it remained there for only three days. One of my friends was given an EBT card worth $292 for groceries, but the funds were only available for October, despite her having lost her job due to the storm and being without an income source. The Asheville communities received recovery funds and assistance freely, while other communities received little or nothing. Smaller, less popular towns had to rely on the kindness of strangers from different cities, states, and even countries.

The current estimates of lives lost range anywhere from 1,000 to 10,000 people from various sources, such as a Search and Rescue representative and a firefighter. Recovery efforts are still finding bodies and body parts. Some believe that some people will never be found. Friends and relatives hold out hope for those missing individuals, but deep in our hearts, we know that they're not coming back. The most disheartening part of the entire situation is the law stating a loved one must be missing for seven years before they can be considered legally deceased. With the power of the raging floodwaters, many have accepted that they will probably never have a loved one's body to lay to rest.

Most of the repairs and environmental clean-up are performed by local civilians. These individuals deserve an award for risking their lives while cleaning up mud and muck that could potentially be contaminated with forever chemicals (PFAS) and radiation. Boots are disintegrating, and cadaver dogs are dropping dead from exposure to chemicals. One would think the government would have supplied Hazmat suits or protective clothing for volunteers, but it hasn't. Residents believe authorities have avoided mentioning hazardous materials to keep the tourists coming to Western North Carolina.

Initially, officials estimated that potable (drinkable) water would not be available in Asheville before mid-December. However, as of November 15, 2024, the date has been moved back to possibly November 20, 2024. Locals suspect that the earlier date has more to do with the upcoming Thanksgiving holiday than it does with reality. The common fear is that locals drank and cooked with dangerous water without realizing it. However, once the water arrived, there was a collective sigh because none of us knew how we would celebrate Thanksgiving with our families if we didn't have potable water. Still, many people continue to consume bottled water out of fear that it may contain chemicals that are not healthy for us. Although the process for cleaning the water was explained ad nauseam, no one trusts that it's 100% safe to drink without consequences. Out of precaution, I've only been drinking bottled water since realizing how dirty the water was when I tried to soak in a bathtub. Honestly, I don't think I'll ever be able to drink tap water again.

When speaking with the locals, most agree that one of the local government's main priorities is getting everything back to normal for tourists. Many fear that the water isn't as clean as it should be due to the various components used in the cleaning process. Those who are still searching for their loved ones believe that both the media and the government are withholding valuable information about the total number of lives lost to save the tourists from hearing all the bad news and deciding not to visit Western North Carolina. Still, others think that FEMA used our disaster area as a stage for the media by not doing anything of value.

A person who wished to remain anonymous described how they watched a "bunch" of FEMA workers sit at a picnic table while locals distributed supplies and tried to clean up debris. Another person described how he was trying to take a generator to an elderly woman in Swannanoa who was on oxygen. However, when he arrived at the location, the police threatened to arrest him if he didn't leave the area immediately. Although stories like this are numerous, it has been challenging to get anyone to go on record for fear of retribution.

Hospitals have struggled to provide potable water to the medical staff for sanitizing equipment, cleaning wounds, and washing their hands with soap. Authorities limited services performed by the Asheville Planned Parenthood clinic and local birthing centers to essential health services due to the lack of running water. Residents suffer exposure to sewage, toxic industrial waste, and mosquito-borne illnesses.[lxxxvii]

Tell me your Hurricane Helene story.

"I live approximately five miles east of Old Fort, North Carolina, and in the days before Helene, weather forecasters were warning of the potential damage Western North Carolina could experience from Hurricane Helene's winds and rain. This immediately prompted a memory of Hurricane Hugo from September 1989. Prior to my move to Old Fort, I lived in Catawba County in the foothills of Western North Carolina. We had warnings about Hugo and the damage in 1989, and we thought then that a hurricane causing damage that far inland was ridiculous, but Hugo came onshore as a Category 4 and proceeded directly inland, over Charlotte, North Carolina, and straight towards Catawba and Iredell counties. We had hundreds of trees down then (many were tall pines native to the area), and no power for seven days following Hurricane Hugo. Fast forward to September 26, 2024. I heeded the warnings! I made sure two of my vehicles were full of fuel, and I had food, water, cat food, batteries, candles, etc., to ride out Helene. My son and I were not prepared for what we saw on September 27, 2024, after Helene."

What did you see on that day?

"We left the house around 11:00 AM to go to Marion, North Carolina, and get some lunch, and what we found was that we were an island in the middle of McDowell County. As we crossed the Catawba River, it was raging! All roads were flooded, the road in front of us (Highway 70) was under 4' of water, and we barely had an LTE cell signal to communicate with our family and friends."

Did you return to the safety of your house?

"We turned around and tried to get to Interstate 40, and it was also flooded at Old Fort. There was a mudslide on Old Fort Mountain, with so many trees almost covering the entirety of Highway 70. Nothing to do but go home and wait out the time with candles and a battery-powered radio."

After the initial shock, did you try to go anywhere else?

"During the five days without power at home, I would drive to a church that is on a hill about a mile away to get a signal to call family and search social media for updates on what was going on with the rest of Western North Carolina. Each day, more and more people would show up at the church to do the same. It was shocking to see on social media what was really going on! Finally, on the third day, I saw Samaritan's Purse drive into the church parking lot with a box truck. Someone finally came to help! Each day was better in some ways and worse in others to hear of what was unfolding in Chimney Rock, Swannanoa, and the River Arts District in Asheville, North Carolina. Almost six months later, it's still hard to digest and see the destruction."

Did you lose anything during the storm?

"My entire refrigerator of food was lost, but I was struggling with 'survivor's guilt' in the weeks after Helene. I had some minor water come through my crawl space and some minor tree damage. It was a bit overwhelming, but my son and pets were my strength. Right now, I'm concerned for others less fortunate than we were."

What message do you want to send to people after this experience?

"No matter how much you may prepare, Mother Nature has plans of her own. Remain calm and prepare as best you can."

Can you describe anything positive from this storm?

"Though our lives and landscapes are changed forever, it's time for new growth and regeneration, personally and in nature. Perhaps where woods and trees once stood, a beautiful park will emerge."

What makes you angry about what happened?

"Some of the posts on social media blaming people for the storm and harassing businesses for not opening."

Are you staying or leaving?

"Why? Staying, I love where I live. The area and its people are resilient, and I want to see what the next 10 years will be like. I want to help where I can. Hashtag WNCSTRONG."

Any suggestions for the government or FEMA?

"Quicker response time."

How did you make a difference during the storm?

"I donated money and food where and when I could. Our neighborhood collected ice, water, and other items when needed for the workers in our area while they were there. I donated time to Sister Kitten to help organize and hand out items to those with pets in need."

Do you wish to mention anyone whom you lost during the storm?

"I lost a friend in the storm when she was trying to rescue her dogs from her home. Her home came off the foundation, and she was swept away in the river. She was found many miles from her home. She was a wonderful supporter of animals and local foster groups."

Main Street – Old Fort, North Carolina

Trucks stranded 3 days on Highway 70 – Old Fort, North Carolina

Flooding by Catawba River at Exit 75 on I-40 – Old Fort, North Carolina

Morganton, North Carolina

CHAPTER TEN

Long Road to Recovery

"There are victims who will never be found, families left to grapple with not having the body of their loved one for closure."

CHAPTER TEN: Long Road to Recovery

People in the South are hard-working, proud people who don't ask for handouts and believe in self-care and independence. However, Hurricane Helene left a path of destruction that residents in every area of Tennessee and North Carolina could feel. Along with job loss, people lost their sources of income in the blink of an eye, and most people don't have a rainy-day fund. Unfortunately, many people live paycheck to paycheck due to the low wages in the service industry. Through this disaster, I have learned that Asheville's cost of living is 5.8 percent higher than the U.S. average and 16.3 percent higher than the North Carolina average. Now, when you realize how much it costs to live comfortably in Asheville (a minimum annual income of $82,080 for a family and $61,600 for a single person),[lxxxviii] think about someone who works in the service industry and their job is closed because there is no potable water for drinking, washing hands, or serving food. Even if your job is open, restaurants require people to pick up food in the drive-thru and eat at home because of the water situation.

Although the City of Asheville is not charging for water during this time, it more than made up for these savings months after the storm. Other businesses aren't being as lenient regarding their bill payments. One Internet provider hasn't been able to supply many customers with Internet coverage for over 29 days. Full payments are still required, and no one knows when they will have Internet again. A few apartment complexes didn't require rent for October, but others sent tenants reminders that rent was still due on the first of the month, regardless of access to potable water.

The local and federal governments have been providing delayed billing, grants, and donations to those affected by Hurricane Helene. However, some haven't accepted the monetary assistance because many people say, "Oh, I don't want to take anything from other people who may need it more." This way of thinking has enabled donations to accumulate, and organizations have been encouraging people to accept help and not be afraid to request assistance. Those of us who did not lose our homes in the flood did try to file for FEMA assistance and received a one-time payment of $750.00. For some people, that's more than what they earn in a week at work. The City of Asheville also offered various grants to musicians, actors, farmers, and others. I applied for assistance as an author and received $500.00 to help cover lost income and marketing expenses for promoting *Butterfly Blossoms by Rachel Bleu*, which I released the day before Hurricane Helene hit North Carolina. Without the Internet and phone service for three weeks, it dampened any sales that could have occurred during those first few days. Access to the Asheville grant allowed me to hire a marketing firm to build my official author website, revise my book cover, and create a book trailer for *Hating Self by Boo Black*.

Residents of Western North Carolina cannot thank people enough for the charitable donations (including money and supplies), hands-on volunteering, and prayers we've received during and after the storm. People have come from all over the United States to help us, including 62 Amish carpenters from Lancaster, Pennsylvania, who built 12 tiny houses in Boone, North Carolina, for the homeless in under 48 hours. A Louisiana-based organization, the Cajun Navy, first volunteered in Florida and then in North Carolina in October 2024 to assist with search and rescue operations, recovery assistance, and supply distribution.

In McDowell County, North Carolina, school buses were used on November 7, 2024, to transport Baxter Healthcare employees to Marion, North Carolina, during Hurricane Helene. Baxter International is a medical supply company that produces 60 percent of the United States' bags of intravenous fluid. They hatched the plan to transport employees before and after school hours. The plant is essential to McDowell County's economy and employs about 2,500 people. Due to flooding from Hurricane Helene, Baxter's closure has caused immediate shortages of IV fluid at hospitals and delayed medical procedures nationwide.[lxxxix]

Many of our local charities have been working tirelessly to provide rental assistance to the community. Grace Covenant Church has already raised and paid rents totaling over $1,000,000. Eblen Charities has increased staff capacity and is processing 40-50 applications a day. Although large amounts of rental assistance are available, it takes time to administer the funds. I can't imagine surviving the flood and then losing my home because of my inability to pay my rent or mortgage. Living in an apartment has many advantages, but no matter where you live, eviction is a reality for many people due to Helene. As with the physical recovery, the emotional scars and trauma run deep, and this experience has ruined the lives of many people by taking away their security and shelter.

Laurrell Jackson-Smith posted the following on her Facebook account, which captures what everyone wants to express: "I want to say that the outpouring of love, support, and supplies to our community has been so amazing, heartfelt, and selfless. The linemen, water workers, K9 search and rescue personnel, construction workers, police officers, and medical staff who gave their lives in other states and countries are truly kind and generous. There are days when I drive around and still cry for my area and my fellow neighbors. I never thought that I would see groups of cadaver dogs. I never thought I would read about entire families swept down the French Broad River. I never thought I would witness the destruction, collective grief, and shock that I am seeing. To say that life is surreal is an understatement. Myself and others who have been affected are suffering from survivor's guilt and shock. Please be kind to anyone you meet who has lived through a disaster. The guilt is awful, and you don't just get over it. There will be years of healing and rebuilding in my community. Some victims will never be found, and families are left to grapple with not having the body of their loved one for closure. The victim count will continue to rise as more are recovered. Homes destroyed, businesses that will never reopen, people who will never be able to start over here in our area, and children who will have to switch schools and leave their friends behind. I cannot even begin to count the missing and found animals that I see on my Facebook feed daily…A phrase I have seen more than once: 'How were they not prepared for this situation?' We live 2,134 feet above sea level in the Appalachian Mountains, and our area is not built to withstand this kind of damage. We are not built for hurricanes; our last major flood was in 1916. We are surrounded by ski resorts and tourists, not beaches and islands. And for the love of God, do not make our tragedy political…I will remain Appalachian strong and will continue to call the mountains my home."[xc]

To assist with the storm recovery efforts, FEMA has offered three ways for homeowners in the flood zone to deal with the loss or damage to their property in Western North Carolina:

1) Acquisition: If your property is severely damaged and is in a flood hazard area, you can apply/sign up for FEMA to buy your home. The value would be the value from the day before the flood. A closing would occur. Then the property would be deeded over to the County, and it would not be able to be reoccupied; it could be converted into parks, greenways, or other public spaces.

2) Elevation: If you had significant water entry, you can apply to FEMA to raise your home. All your possessions stay in place, you move into a hotel, and you return to a home that is newly 2 feet above the 100-year flood. I'm not clear on what that means for a 1000-year flood level; they reiterated that they use the 100-year flood level and add 2'.

3) Mitigation Reconstruction: If it is determined that your home cannot be safely elevated to the new height, you can apply to have your home destroyed and rebuilt with a standard floor plan home. You would have to move out, and FEMA would help coordinate that process, too.[xci]

Before we can completely recover, we must face the fact that homelessness has become an ongoing concern throughout Western North Carolina. Homelessness has always been an issue due to the influx of transient populations flocking to areas that provide financial assistance and a place to call home. However, following Helene, more residents are experiencing homelessness because of the loss of their homes or the uninhabitable condition of their homes due to water damage and mold. As of April 5, 2025, the U.S. Department of Housing and Urban Development reported that 1,548 people affected by Hurricane Helene are sheltered in hotels and motels.[xcii]

Another concern is the increase in the property tax cost during storm recovery. "Buncombe County's proposed spending plan will require a property tax hike, which will include a 3.26-cent property tax increase, raising the rate by 6% to 55.02 cents per $100 of assessed value. The increase would net the county an estimated $17.1 million next fiscal year."xciii Homeowners were already struggling with the affordability of living in Western North Carolina, especially in and around the Asheville area. Hurricane Helene has placed additional stress on those homeowners because they are footing the bill for the storm's destruction.

Additional concerns pertain to the French Broad and Swannanoa Rivers. "On May 7, 2025, the National Trust for Historic Preservation named the French Broad and Swannanoa River Corridors on the 2025 list of America's 11 Most Endangered Historic Places."xciv The list is compiled to heighten awareness about the threats facing the nation's greatest treasures. Inclusion in the list will provide much-needed national attention and support to Western North Carolina communities. The bigger question is what other parts of Western North Carolina have been so greatly affected or decimated that human intervention in the future will be necessary to prevent them from being added to the endangered list.

CHAPTER ELEVEN

Mental and Physical Health

"We should not have people freezing in tents because they are unhoused."

CHAPTER ELEVEN: Mental & Physical Health

The road to recovery would not be complete without mentioning the mental health of the volunteers involved in the recovery, the first responders, and the victims of Helene. Mental Health providers have been available at many care stations throughout North Carolina. However, with the stigma attached to mental conditions, I'm not sure how many people have taken advantage of the offer for help. Add to that the mountain-folk idea of taking care of yourself and standing on your own two feet, and you have an additional roadblock to healing.

Worse yet, survivor's guilt has gotten hold of me. Every day, I wake up thinking about what has occurred, and I am still in shock from what I've seen and experienced firsthand. No matter what you may have heard, the devastation is much worse than reported by the media. Not everyone can handle everything that has happened, so they keep quiet. At one point, misinformation was a frequent topic, and many people didn't believe there were bodies found in trees, even though they could believe that an 18-wheeler could be stuck in a tree. I've talked to multiple witnesses who have seen the bodies in the trees. Not witnessing the event doesn't make it untrue. I have painted a vivid picture in my mind of this event and can't unsee those bodies. For some reason, if someone doesn't see something with their own eyes, they claim it is fake news or a lie. I cannot think of a single person or reason for anyone to invent such a disturbing story. Those of us who lived through the storm are in no way able to create untruths for entertainment because we're still in shock from the traumatic experience. If you choose not to believe the information within these pages, I have no magical potion or words to change your mind, but know that I have no reason to lie or make up stories. I don't want to face the reality of everything and everyone we have lost. I want so badly for life to go back to normal and the way that it was before Hurricane Helene destroyed our security and our home.

The primary purpose of this book is to discuss the resiliency of communities as they focus on finding their new normal and becoming stronger than ever. I see that, but I fear that months of disappointment and frustration will make us lose momentum. Mountain people are a strong breed of people who can do anything they put their minds to, but I worry about their mental health. The stress of losing loved ones is overwhelming, and they will never forget them. We will continue to mourn, and there is no timetable for how long you mourn a loved one. For this reason, we need access to mental health counselors for everyone.

Although there have been some mental health professionals at the care stations, many people don't believe in counseling. People say they're fine and refuse to seek help. Depression and suicide don't always show obvious symptoms, and it's something that touches many of us. What happens after a few months of dealing with the pain of loss and the compounding stress? Will some people contemplate ending their lives? Trying to stay optimistic about the situation, I still can't forget the story about the driver on Interstate 40 who ignored the road closure signs. The driver drove around the signs and then plummeted down an embankment, landing in the water below. Miraculously, they rescued the driver, but she later died in the hospital. Later, authorities confirmed that the driver had attempted suicide. What did this woman experience? Did she lose her entire family, her husband, or her child? What was the final straw that pushed her to end it all? Unfortunately, there are no answers to these questions.

Through Hurricane Helene Resiliency After the Storm, I aim to raise awareness about the importance of mental health, self-care, and community support. I also want everyone to remember that they're not alone. We've all experienced something horrible, and we're all going to handle it differently. Our memories of Hurricane Helene will remain with us for a very long time, if not forever. For this reason, I am including a list below of the symptoms that may alert you to seek help from a counselor or medical professional:

- "Big personality changes, eating, or sleeping patterns.

- An inability to cope with problems or daily activities.

- Lack of connection with or withdrawal from daily activities.

- Exaggerated beliefs or thinking that's not reality-based.

- A large amount of fear or nervousness.

- Lasting feelings of sadness, helplessness, or hopelessness.

- Thoughts or statements about suicide or harming others.

- Problems with drinking, smoking, or using drugs.

- Large mood swings.

- A lot of anger or hostility.

- Violent behavior."[xcv]

Western North Carolina was fortunate that the Federal Emergency Management Agency provided free crisis counseling and mental health support for impacted residents of Helene. The goal was to help survivors develop stress management and coping skills, as well as access additional resources. They delivered these services to residents' inaccessible locations, including survivors' homes, shelters, temporary living sites, and places of worship.[xcvi]

When I'm driving to work, I often gaze at my surroundings. Many things look different. I'm not seeing houses that have washed away because, in my area, there aren't any. I have seen some businesses that are no longer there. The main thing I'm noticing is the piles of debris. On my right, I can see piles of leaves, tree limbs, and an innumerable number of plastic bags hanging from the trees. When I reach Brevard Road and the French Broad River, I can see the unnatural waterline on the right side of the mountain. On the left, I can see where all the trash and debris have collected in the tops of trees. Hundreds of trees have fallen, some completely uprooted from their homes.

We're fifty-plus days from the storm, and many areas are still waiting for assistance. It looks the same, as if a bomb had been dropped. The top priority is to get people off the streets before a major snowstorm causes another catastrophe. The local governments constantly ask for volunteers to help clean up downtown Asheville. However, the mud is toxic and mixed with chemicals, and some stories have mentioned radiation. Multiple stories discuss how people's work boots are disintegrating and falling apart. Why would anyone want to volunteer under these circumstances and in such hazardous conditions? Some people have thrown caution to the wind and are risking their lives to help get Western North Carolina back on track.

When I think about 911 workers and all the first responders who risked their lives, many are dead because they selflessly gave of themselves and volunteered their time to help. In their minds, they were volunteering their time, but they were unknowingly sacrificing their lives. I am concerned about the long-term effects of exposure to mud and any other substances mixed in with the mud. The locals have told me that back in the 1960s, one business produced lithium batteries and disposed of the hazardous waste chemicals. A larger problem is that, wherever they stored those barrels underground, they disappeared after Hurricane Helene. It's terrifying to think about where the barrels went. People say that years ago, companies dumped the chemicals into our soil and water.

On our journey of resilience and renewal, regret will become a central theme as we progress through the recovery. I still wonder why the authorities didn't take the missing chemicals and contaminants more seriously. FEMA or the local government should have had the volunteers outfitted in protective suits and breathing apparatuses for safety precautions. So many people have lost their jobs and don't have medical insurance, so if they become sick, they're going to pile into hospitals, and they can't turn away those sick from contamination. In return, the medical expenses of Helene victims will explode to cover the uninsured or underinsured.

Will we ever return to normal? Will we have assistance available when people are exposed to contaminants in the mud and water? Although I try not to be political, I believe the blame rests with ALL politicians on both sides. Our representatives vote to give themselves annual raises and have substantial salaries. But we have people who are homeless and living in tents, hotels, and cars. There are unemployed people without necessities and hope. Reflect on how the government has addressed our needs in Western North Carolina. FEMA representatives have been on site and have tried to help by providing care stations for washing clothes, bathing, and distributing supplies. A few of us were able to complete an application and receive $750 and hotel vouchers for a few days. However, the things we require most, the government has failed to provide. The money deducted from our paychecks for taxes is supposed to help ALL of us in emergencies, and these politicians hold the purse strings. Unfortunately, our politicians are so far removed from the situation that they have no idea how their decisions affect us. Or, if they do know, they do not seem to care as much as they should.

Too many times, we've been told, "Our prayers are with you." Well, prayers don't pay the bills, they don't house the homeless, and they aren't going to get us to where we need to be in the next five to ten months. The bottom line is we need more financial assistance. Yes, grants are available; however, people without Internet access cannot apply. Many people lack access to or the ability to use a computer, making it difficult for them to apply for a grant or FEMA assistance. Does anyone realize that people are waiting on hold for over an hour to speak with a FEMA representative? Who has time to wait that long? My emotions are raw, and I feel anger and disgust at our situation. I'm angry because the only reason some of us can go back to work is not because of the government's assistance, but because of the mountain people, Appalachian people, and all the people with chainsaws who went out during and after the storm to cut trees so that we could drive out and get supplies. Regular people in the community drove out with their big hearts and did whatever they felt needed to be done.

The government arrived days later and preached to the media about what they provided for us, but other people had already done the hard work. The government flew in and took credit for it all, granting interviews, having photo ops, and providing kind words to make us believe they cared. Some people did care. The Wells Fargo Care Station in Candler had volunteers from Alabama and Georgia, and they were amazing. Giving up their everyday lives to help people they didn't even know, they were a bright and shining light for those of us struggling to survive. The high-level individuals who make the decisions and receive huge paychecks just want to look good. If they genuinely cared, they would have rolled up their sleeves and joined their employees.

Sitting around without the internet and electricity led to an epiphany. Why couldn't the government have distributed gift cards to everyone instead of requiring us to apply online for $750? Not everyone had electricity, so we could use the gift cards once the power was restored. Gift cards could have been used for medicine, groceries, and clothing. Why was this not an option? Cold, hard cash would have been the best option for us, but then we would have needed armed guards to keep us safe. Or they could have mailed the gift cards or even checks to us? I've seen many people here who are too prideful to even go to the care stations to ask for help. They keep saying that other people are worse off. People are so prideful that they don't want to ask for help, and I don't understand their mindset. Sometimes, we must be willing to ask for help. If you're always a giver, you must also learn to be a taker when times are desperate. Now is that time.

"In many areas hit by flooding, homes were left isolated by damaged roads and bridges. Contaminated water is one of the leading health risks, but residents also face harm to mental health, stress that exacerbates chronic diseases, and several other threats. Floodwater with sewage or other harmful contaminants in it can lead to infectious diseases, particularly among people who are already ill, immunocompromised, or have open wounds. Even after the water recedes, residents may underestimate the potential for contamination by unseen bacteria, such as fecal coliform, heavy metals like lead, and organic and inorganic contaminants, including pesticides. Inside homes, floodwater can create more health risks, particularly if mold grows on wet fabrics and wallboards. Standing water outside also increases the risk of exposure to mosquitoes carrying diseases such as West Nile virus. Cuts and other injuries are common in the aftermath of storms, as people clean up debris, and even small wounds can become infected. The stress, exertion, and exposure to heat can also exacerbate chronic conditions such as cardiovascular and respiratory diseases."[xcvii]

Whether people became ill from accidentally consuming water from toothbrushing, eating off washed utensils, or inadvertently drinking the contaminated water, gastrointestinal cases have continued to rise. "Flooded sewers always produce some degree of overflow. The sewage mixes into creeks, manholes, and wells, producing a dangerous soup of bacteria. Highly contagious illnesses like cholera, salmonella, and norovirus can flourish in such conditions; all of these can cause diarrhea, vomiting, and dehydration that can severely sicken and even kill the immunocompromised, elderly, and very young."[xcviii] In the following interview, we learned that something as simple as going to the creek for water can harm even healthy individuals.

What were you doing the day of the storm?

"I was at home, but I had driven back from Myrtle Beach the day before, and I remember seeing the storm rolling in at the beach. There was a ton of water, and I remember thinking the beach was going to get slaughtered. As I hit the mountains, the rain was coming down in absolute sheets, coming across Old Fort Mountain. I get home and check on my family, and we're all good. and then school gets called off for the next two days. We went to bed the next night, but when I woke up, I didn't know anything had happened overnight because we live in a brick house and hadn't heard anything. I remember waking up, and my phone was ringing and ringing, and my dad kept calling me, and he kept cutting out, and he asked me if I was okay. My stepdaughter's family was calling me, too. Finally, I got a quick call through to everyone and said we were fine but that I hadn't surveyed the damage."

How did you prepare?

"Well, living in the mountains, we do get hurricane winds and rains every year. It's completely normal for my kids to miss one to three days of school on average due to debris on the roads and flooding. We had water, non-perishable items, but unfortunately, in a situation like this, where you go sometimes weeks without electricity and water, it's really hard to prepare, but I'll tell you the steps we took after the storm. We live on a well, so we knew our well wouldn't work. We had plenty of food and water for us and our animals. Flushing toilets were the main concern. My boys were 10 and 13 at the time. [She paused to collect herself as painful memories came flooding back.] We reside in the country and would go down to the creek every day, and we had old cat litter containers to fill up with water to flush toilets. My youngest son, because of using creek water, ended up with an infection in the skin around his knee. You don't hear of that in 2024, getting an infection from hauling creek water."

What damages did you suffer?

"The damage was minimal; peanuts compared to the water other people suffered. We have an above-ground pool, so the lining got ripped out. A pipe going into the house got ripped out, and insurance isn't the greatest about paying for such things. A section of our fence got taken out by our neighbor's tree falling on it. The day the hurricane went through, my partner, Chris, is a landscaper, and he asked me to drive around and see which neighbors needed help, so my kids and I got in the car to drive around and find victims that needed help."

Do you personally know anyone lost in the storm?

"I do not know anyone personally, but working in Buncombe County Schools, we did have three students who were killed. The first little boys were swept away with his mom and dad by the Toe River. They were trying to escape and prepared, and as they got in their car, it started to float. They got out, and a witness saw a wave take all four of them down the river. Another one perished with his grandparents after a roof collapsed, but the mom survived. No, I didn't know them personally, but as someone who works with schools, I count on seeing my little babies' faces every day of the week. I work at the school for those kids. I can't imagine how any educator and their little friends felt after not seeing those kids there. It absolutely destroys me to think about. We [educators] think of the kids as our own, and they are ours for a year. All my kids at my school were safe, and I just needed to hug every one of them. And, I will say that Buncombe County schools did an amazing job taking care of their staff.

You didn't ask me this question, but I want to vent about something. I hate all the stupid rumors that went around. It was so unnecessary. Saying that Mission Hospital had like 500 bodies, but their morgue holds like 60 at the most. Yes, there were refrigerated trucks that were brought in just in case we needed them, but those rumors hurt people and gave them unnecessary stress."

How did you help others in your community?

"My partner [Chris] is a self-employed landscaper, and every day I went out and I found people that needed help in our community, as far as like removing trees from their driveway and clearing debris. WE live in a rural area and have a ton of neighbors. Chris and others went out and helped others clear debris and trees. Two ladies had two trees fall through their room, and Chris and his employee went over and cleared everything off so the ladies could survey the water. We had an extra case of water, so my two boys and I drove around handing out water and wrote down names of local radio stations where they could get information, told them where HOTSPOTS were, so people could contact families. In all seriousness, I'm really proud of my community, and this was an unprecedented event, and I pray to God it never happens again. For a community that never had anything like this happen, I think we did really good as a community and helped one another. Every day I turned on the radio, the Buncombe County Manager [Avril Pender] was telling us what was going on twice a day. I know a lot of people from the outside are unhappy with the response, but our last massive flood was in 1916, and at least we were able to communicate [before the storm] and somewhat prepare. I don't know that you can fully prepare for one of the deadliest hurricanes or ask your government to be fully prepared for things that don't normally happen."

Do you have any advice for someone who may be faced with a natural disaster?

"Have plenty of water, non-perishables, if you can afford it, a generator, and give yourself grace because things may happen that are completely out of your control. Be graceful, patient, and calm. Stay as freaking calm as you can. I am currently in therapy for this situation for the survivor's guilt and PTSD, and I'm not ashamed to tell you. It's okay to get help if they need it. People need to know it's okay to get help and seek out professional help if you are hurting and don't know how to handle the situation. It's okay because how can you handle a crazy situation like this?"

What are your thoughts about Western North Carolina following the storm?

"I was not born in Asheville. My mother and her side of the family, though, have lived in Buncombe County for well over 150 years. All my family has been born at Mission Hospital, but I'm the oddball. I was born in Wilmington because my dad was in the Air Force. Asheville has always been my home because my family is here. And to see it broke my heart, and it still breaks my heart. Driving around and seeing the aftermath. Just picturing families living in the areas that were destroyed by the storm is heartbreaking. Driving around and seeing the aftermath, I believe that the government should be doing more. We should not have people freezing in tents because they are unhoused; that is ludicrous to me. Seeing people being sent a hotel voucher for a hotel two hours away instead of fixing their plumbing or helping them find a permanent place to stay is stupid to me. Homeowners' insurance is giving them less than half the value of the homes they paid for. I feel like insurance is the vultures, and they're going to do awful things to people in our area. They denied claims for home damage because it wasn't covered under their policy. Not giving people flood insurance unless they're in a designated floodplain and live on the river. It's the aftermath, in my opinion, that is the absolute worst; it's collateral damage. I think we're going to feel this for years to come."

What was the scariest part of the entire ordeal?

"One of the scariest things for me was waking up the morning after the catastrophe and not knowing what had happened or not knowing what our area looked like. I had people calling me, almost panicked, to see if I was okay. I had zero idea of what was going on around me. It was a surreal feeling to be in the middle of a catastrophe or disaster zone and not know what was going on around you."

Alexander, North Carolina

CHAPTER TWELVE

Local Heroes

"I always believed in my heart that all things happen for a reason. You don't know why, but somewhere down the road, it was meant to be."

CHAPTER TWELVE: Local Heroes

Without the dedication and tenacity of local heroes, the situation in Western North Carolina would have been significantly worse. No one realizes they're a hero until the time calls for one. I have spoken to many people who have prepared meals for neighbors, allowed strangers to shower and wash clothes in their homes, and provided shelter and supplies to those in need. Although I have many stories I'd like to share, the individuals involved don't feel that they did anything that someone else wouldn't have done. Not wanting any praise or unnecessary attention, I have only been able to mention such stories. However, the following pages will provide examples of how ordinary people became superheroes and made a difference in people's lives.

Tunnel Road - Asheville, North Carolina

Tunnel Road - Asheville, North Carolina

COLEY DUFFIE & CODY WARD OF THE CHAINSAW BROTHERS
– Bethel, North Carolina

Are you from Western North Carolina?

Coley: "I just moved back about a month before the storm. I'm a cross-breed, North Georgia, and here, but this has always been my home. Spent most of my childhood here until I was 12, and then my family moved to Georgia and then moved back a few times throughout the years. I just moved back, and I'm here to for good."

Cody: "I'm a native, born and raised here."

What were you guys doing the day of the storm?

Coley: "We went to Bryson City because we knew it was going to get kinda bad, and so our families loaded up and stayed there Saturday and came back here Monday morning. We bought a bunch of generators, and we didn't have any power, but by the time we hooked them up, the power came back on. Canton wasn't as bad as with Hurricane Fred three years ago. That's where Cody lost everything."

Cody: "All I had left was my wife's car after Fred. I was living in the Caruso area, which is actually Bethel."

Coley: "So, we came back and the power came on, but we didn't have no cell service and no Wi-Fi, but once we came over Blossom Mountain, there was like a million cars on the side of the road and we were like, 'What the heck is going on?' Everybody was going over there to get phone service. But our boss was telling us we weren't going to have any work for three or four weeks because he didn't want to repo cars, and parents were staying with their kids at Western Carolina University because of the storm. Cody looked at me and said, 'I didn't get no help after Hurricane Fred. We gotta do something.'

Fred lost everything, and all he had was a pair of socks. We were listening to the radio about we heard about Holly. She called in about her mom, and the tree companies were trying to take advantage of her. I was like, 'Let's go help them out.' Cody called his dad and asked if we could borrow a chainsaw and a truck, and my buddy came up from Georgia. So, we went over there to help Holly's mom, and there were three guys actually doing the easy work to get paid, but they wouldn't do the one problem tree. It was a big one. Holly explained that she'd given the last $900 she had to them, and we said, 'We're not taking any money, we're just doing this and helping people,' and she still made us take $100, which helped because we had to buy a new chain and bar for the chainsaw. And that's just kinda how it started. And the next thing you know, the radio station was dispatching us to people to go, the bad ones, big trees on houses."

Cody: "We'd get gas and take gas jugs and generators, and go and charge phones and put gas in their cars and talk to them. Stuff like that."

Coley: "If people donated money, we donated it back. For months, if people gave us money, we'd give it back. Like, there was a single-wide trailer and a massive red oak fell, and they lost everything. They said, 'We're going to bulldoze it and hopefully get a new house. I just want to get in there and see what I do have left. If you can just get it off my house and cut me a way in.' We told them this is why we do this. That's why we take donations, so you don't have to worry about this, but they gave us one of the biggest donations, and they would not let us go. That's the way it was. I've never seen this community come together like it did during this storm. If it weren't for the radio station, there'd be so many people lost. I believe in the first few months, we helped over 140 people, and we were just a small group of guys. But now we're a business and have three full-time guys, and we've got a couple of contract guys we use. We stay small, but the more people you hire, the more you have to worry about. Our main goal is not about making money; it's about taking care of the people in Western North Carolina that we can. A lot of people don't want to do jobs that are difficult. So, we're doing everything that no one else wants to do."

Cody: "We got the bottom of the barrel."

If someone needed to contact you, how would they reach you?

Coley: "We have a Facebook account. Look under The Chainsaw Brothers [*Coley and Cody are actually cousins*], but that name came from the radio station (99.9 Country FM). We are an official business now. We're not staying months out; we're just picking and choosing jobs. Like, I just left a job over here in Leicester, an older gentleman who's been in his house 45 years, raised all his kids there, and he's older now and dealing with a lot of health issues. He's worried about his wife having to deal with all that, so I went out to look. He said, 'I'm not sure I can afford it, but I'd really like to have all this taken care of, but I don't know if I can afford it.' I said, 'We're going to do it regardless of your financial issues. We'll just do it for a daily rate, but that's what we're trying to do.' We're not trying to get the spotlight, but he doesn't want to leave his wife with a problem, and it wasn't even storm-related, but that's the name of the game. That's why we continue doing what we're doing, because it feels good. I knew that even after the storm, we'd be able to help people like that."

So, what phone number can they use to reach The Chainsaw Brothers?

Coley: "828-316-1013."

Did you guys personally lose anything with the storm?

Both: "We were golden. We were blessed."

Coley: "We were high enough not to have any problems, and that's exactly why I feel like that happened for a reason."

Cody: "We got a bunch of trees around our house, and none of those trees fell or nothing."

Coley: "Massive white oaks and the fact that none of them fell. After seeing what we've seen."

What's the worst thing that you've seen?

Coley: "We pulled up on some places that looked like an atomic bomb went off."

Cody: "Entire houses that you had to cut your way in."

Coley: "As far as actual damage to house and property, the worst was probably the first one we called into the radio station about and asked for help. This oak at the base was 8-9 feet around, and it was massive. It was laid across the whole house, and they lost the garage, two cars, I mean, it was bad, and that was actually when we met some of the other chainsaw brothers, like Justin and Billy. And one of the ones that will always stand out to us forever was over here in Leicester, a lady and her husband had just built this nice porch on the front of their house, and had been spending years remodeling the inside, and they had a Christmas tree that was 37 years old. It was her son's first Christmas tree."

It wasn't Kandy, was it? She mentioned her tree and sent photos.

Coley: "Yes, it was. Did she show you the plaque? We had that made for her with her son's name on it. We cut a piece of the tree that fell and had it made for her. She came to the radio station, and that's when we gave it to her."

It's dangerous work that you guys are doing.

Coley: "Yes, it takes a special type of person to do the work we're doing. We have a bucket truck, too, that raises you up to the trees. I had a guy in Henderson County who had a tree he wanted us to look at, so it was a little bigger and it was bigger than what we wanted to take on at the time, but he had a friend named Larry who owned a bucket truck that he rented out from time to time. I asked if I could come out and look at it, but he said it wasn't running right now. I told him I still wanted to see it, so when I got there, I was able to get the truck to run for 37 seconds exactly, and then it would cut off. He agreed to sell it to me and allowed us to work out payment arrangements. If it wasn't for him, we probably wouldn't be who we are today. He gave us a chance when no one else would. We've been blessed. If it wasn't for Western North Carolina, we wouldn't be here."

You've turned into heroes. You were our lifeline.

Coley: "People would tell us, 'We listen to y'all every morning and every night on the radio.' Every morning, we'd call in and get what we needed to work on and then talk to Mark and Eddie at the radio station. Then we'd call in at night and give an update to those guys. It was like a theme show."

Are you being profitable yet?

Coley: "Not yet. We're paying our bills, and we're not losing anything. We're just trying to do what's right. We might do one job where we make money and another job where we lose money, but it kind of evens out. It will probably be profitable in about 5 years."

How are you dealing with the mental health part of this?

Coley: "We just keep working. Cody has a break at the end of June. I just took a couple of days off. We just don't stop. We've been going strong since the storm happened. I don't think we've actually sat down and thought about all that we've done. Seeing all the things that people have dealt with and how they're handling it. If you go on our Facebook page, some of the reviews that people give us kinda say what we need to know, and that we are doing enough. I guess that helps us cope with what they went through. It will never replace all that everyone has lost. The biggest thing that hits home with me is I've worked a lot of storms for a living, and people talk about all that they lost, but this storm was different. But people here in this community, it was, 'I'm alive. I've got this, and I can rebuild this. I helped my neighbors. When I lost everything, I was over there cutting a tree off my neighbor's house.' That right there is what gave me all the hope that I needed. And it told me that we're still in a time when people matter. That gave us hope. I say all the time that Western North Carolina is totally different."

Do you have any advice for people who made it through the storm unscathed?

Coley: "Do anything you can to get the hazard away from your house, even if it's just trimming it. Tree maintenance has to be done. Most of the trees that went down were big, heavy oaks. There are things you can do, and these trees are still wind-shook and not settled because of all the wind and rain that we've had. A lot of stuff happened to people, and we don't need to forget that. The people who were unscathed will never understand unless they knew someone or volunteered. We are all together as one."

<u>Where were you on the day of the storm?</u>

Woody: "I was here at home the day before the storm. I've been through flooding a couple of times, and the water has come up, but never as far up as this time. Last time, I had to renovate the whole house because the water was knee-deep. It's a relatively small creek, but when it rains and water gets up, it gets out and it's a monster. We call it Mud Creek, but the official name is the Oklawaha. But everybody calls it Mud Creek. It goes to the other side of the county [Henderson] and is one of the major creeks around here."

Mud Creek (Oklawaha) - Hendersonville, North Carolina

Bobby: "The pasture always floods first around the bridge. To be safe, Woody drove 15 miles and stayed with his daughter the night before the flooding got too bad.

That night, a transformer went through Woody's car window around 7:00 the next morning. He stayed with his daughter for about a week. My wife and I got flooded out and couldn't get out and check on Woody because the water was up over that bridge, and you couldn't even see the bridge. The trailers in the Kimberly Clark loading dock got turned over. The water got to the eaves of Woody's house. When it started flooding, a neighbor took a picture before it covered his house."

Woody's House 3 Days before Helene - Hendersonville, North Carolina

Woody's House 1 Day before Helene - Hendersonville, North Carolina

Berkley Road – Hendersonville, North Carolina

Country Music Hall of Fame, Don Gibson's Car - Woody Won in Auction

<u>Were you able to save anything before the house completely flooded?</u>

Woody: "I tried to get as much small stuff as I could, but it was pouring rain, and I was able to get my guns."

Bobby: "He loves the three G's: golf, God, and guns. I came over here, and it was a disaster, and I wanted to find his golf clubs. I found his nine-wood, and I told him if he ever passed away, I was going to put that nine-wood in with him. So, we came over here two or three days later, after the water receded. I went back into the house and started lifting things up, and that's when I found the clubs. I took the clubs out of the bags and cleaned them with soap and water, and threw away the golf bag. So, days later, Woody said he wanted to play but that he didn't have any clubs, so I told him I had some he could borrow. He will write two green marks on his ball because every golfer will put something on their balls so that he knows which one is theirs. So, I got 24 balls and made green marks on them like his, and got new tees and towels, so we met up at Dunham Hills Golf Course to play. He kept saying he didn't know if he could play with someone else's clubs. He had no idea I had his clubs. He walked over and looked in the trunk, and said, 'Are those my clubs?' He came over and hugged me and lifted me up, and he had a great round of golf because they were his clubs. We've been friends for 28 years."

Woody's Golf Clubs Recovered by Bobby

Has the government or FEMA been helpful since you lost your entire home?

Woody: "No insurance help at all. Some FEMA help, but nothing that comes close to home replacement."

How prepared were you for the storm?

Woody: "You just don't ever know. It's happened before, and it floods to the top of the bank. Whatever the good Lord lets happen. It's never happened, and I never thought it would be up to the eaves of the house."

Bobby: "Years ago, the water only got up to knee-level. It was 2004 hurricanes Frances and Ivan where the house had to be remodeled. Your safe place is your home."

How long did you live in the house?

Woody: "Probably twenty-five years."

Bobby: "His mom and dad owned the house, and Woody grew up in this house. But when he got older, he stayed up in the mobile home setting up behind the house. It's about 25 feet above where the house was sitting."

Bobby: "The picture of the flooding on the eaves of the house is from a trail-cam."

Woody: "The water was up over the road."

Trail Cam of Woody's House - Hendersonville, North Carolina

How long did it take for the water to move out and get back to the creek?

Woody: "Probably four or five days to go down, but to get back to normal, probably a week or longer."

What was the older man who stopped in the truck talking about when he mentioned some mobile homes floated away?

Woody: "There were a couple of mobile homes going down North Main, and where it crosses I-26. The people refused to evacuate, and the water took them away."

Where have you been living since your house had to be demolished?

Woody: "I've been staying with my sister, but the church and the Amish donated a tiny home, a cooler, bedding, and a tin tub for bathing."

What about a bathroom or toilet?

Woody: "You'd have to just go outside, but I've got my sister's home."

Do you have any advice for people?

Woody: "Be prepared. You've got to have food, water, any necessities that you may not be able to get to if you're trapped."

Was your sister prepared?

Woody: "Yes, she was prepared and she was on higher ground, so that made a difference. The wind and rain were pretty bad, but there were gale-force winds and it was windy and rainy."

What helped you get through everything?

Woody: "God. My dad was a preacher all his life, and I was a preacher's kid. I always believed in my heart that all things happen for a reason. You don't know why, but somewhere down the road, it was meant to be, and things happen for a reason. The good Lord puts things out there, and they may change a part of our lives."

Are you planning to rebuild your home?

Woody: "No, I'm going to move the old mobile home on the hill, and I've ordered a new mobile home to place up in the same spot. I will not put anything back down where the house was, so I'll be about 28 feet above where the house was."

Woody's Demolished Home - Hendersonville, North Carolina

Location of Demolished House - Hendersonville, North Carolina

<u>Do you think that will keep you safe if there's another storm?</u>

Woody: "Yes. I've been here all my life, and it's never been that bad. It's gotten maybe halfway or three-quarters of the way up the bank."

<u>What does that mean for the land down here?</u>

Woody: "This land is low-lying, and I used to always have animals down here like horses, sheep, mules, and dogs. At some point and time, I may get another dog, but I'm not sure what would happen if it flooded again."

<u>Is there anything you would like people to know about your experience?</u>

Woody: "Be close-knit with your family and friends and take care of each other because when it comes down to it, that's all we've got. When you've got your friends and your family, you can get through anything, and the good Lord. Things happen for a reason, and the devil tries to tempt and test you. We know who's in charge."

Papa's and Beers off Asheville Highway - Hendersonville, North Carolina

Broadmoor Golf Course, Four Months before Helene - Fletcher, North Carolina

Broadmoor Golf Course after Helene - Fletcher, North Carolina

One Disaster from Homelessness

"People were scared and there was a sense or feeling of panic all around us."

CHAPTER THIRTEEN: One Disaster from Homelessness

Months following Hurricane Helene, reports indicate that over 12,000 people lost their homes due to the storm. Governments made promises that remain unkept. For example, a fund created for 1,000 temporary housing trailers resulted in only six being completed and assigned. Agencies assigned to assist victims have fallen short of helping the most vulnerable. In one story, an agency that was responsible for finding homes for the displaced refused to help one victim because their credit score was too low.

It is unfortunate that society still labels the homeless population as either too lazy, too crazy, or addicts of some form or fashion. Truth be told, many are just like you and me, and every person's situation is different. Regardless of the cause, each individual deserves kindness, respect, and understanding. As human beings, we should be the first ones to acknowledge the pain and suffering of our fellow neighbors and lend a helping hand. Hurricane Helene has shed a bright light on the reality that homelessness can affect anyone. Each of us is one disaster or one medical misfortune away from losing everything and ending up on the streets. No one chooses to live on the streets or in their vehicle. Too many people make judgments about the homeless and choose to pretend that they don't exist. They do exist, and sadly, one day, that person could be you. In Western North Carolina, the cost of living is so great that many people must share an apartment or house to make ends meet. In the following interview, you will see how easily homelessness can sneak into your life.

Tell us your Hurricane Helene story.

Brittany: "We were living at our Asheville apartment and saw on the news that a storm was coming, but we had no idea of the depth of the situation. I remember watching the news, and then the next day we woke up and all the alarms were sounding all over the apartment complex, no electricity, but we were on a high floor, so we were fine. The kids were with us. The elevators were out, so that was difficult. As the day wore on, we started seeing the Chinook helicopters and different air rescue planes come through. The one thing that was the most shocking was the silence in the beginning, and then the nonstop alarms. And, I don't think we understood at that moment exactly how bad things were. I think it was three or four days before we ventured out to try to find food."

David: "It was the second day that I went out to go to my job and see what was going on. It was complete chaos. Everybody was throwing everything away because all the power had gone out for six or seven hours, and I was working as the Assistant Manager in the meat department at a local grocery store. When I got there, they were throwing everything away, saying everything went bad and the trucks were flooded out, so nothing was coming in, and no job to work at. So, my decision was to start getting supplies for my family, and that's the point that I lost my job. I was already on FMLA for my health, so they knew I was sick and starting renal failure (due to Lupus), but I can't go to work because I'm constantly on dialysis."

Brittany: "And so, whenever you're facing something really bad, rent and bills are not on your mind. What's on your mind is we've got these two little boys, and how are you going to take care of these kids?"

David: "It was a month later when I got sick and had to go on dialysis, which I go to three times a week."

Brittany: "We spent our time going up and down stairs because there was no elevator, and we were on the fourth floor. There was another disabled person, and she only had one working arm and had to go without the elevator and haul stuff up. A lot of people who had the money to get out of the apartments were gone, and they left. Over time, you could smell food rotting from the apartments and coming out into the hallways. We spent every day going out and sourcing bottled water.

The first people to help us was Ross Farm on Holbrook Road. Ross Farm provided the first drinkable water, and they gave people free five-gallon buckets and went to the creek and filled it for anyone to use for their toilets.
We also met an Asheville artist there who stopped to get water, and he turns plastic bottles into art around the area. He gave us some of his plastic containers so we could get more water.

Then, we went out to take my mom some Sophia water and left a plate with a note to my mom telling her that Elon Musk was going to provide Starlink because we didn't have internet and any way of contacting anyone. My mom is disabled."

David: "My mom lives in Weaverville, and I had no idea whether she was okay or not. Reems Creek was completely destroyed out there, so I was worried to death about them. I had distant family in Georgia that was trying to reach out and couldn't get hold of anybody. So, everyone was in complete distress."

Brittany: "So, I left a plate with the few supplies I could. On our way back through, there were these children and their parents set up where people could grab one of their five-gallon buckets, and they were scooping up water from the creek with these buckets and giving them to people. They also had clean, potable water, and that got us through, and we went back there twice. Whenever I could post and the Internet was working, I would tell others about any help we received and where to go."

David: "There's a place on Sardis Road called Best Buy Metals, and they were giving out hamburgers and a case of water and chips, and it was so awesome. That was the first warm meal in seven days."

Brittany: "We were out in our truck getting water, and on several of those trips, our children came with us and helped us get stuff. I think we were most worried at the time about what they would see, and that was a concern I had. I know that after growing up in a traumatic childhood, things like that stick with you. I would assume it's the same with a disaster. Seeing the infrastructure of our city torn to pieces. I hurt my foot and rolled it a couple of times carrying stuff up the stairs. It was about a month after doing the supply runs that we finally got working elevators. No one at that rental property was there. They did not show up to check on anyone. There was nothing. David started having issues and couldn't breathe or get out of bed. It was our son's 13th birthday party in August, and at that point, David wasn't getting out of bed that well."

David: "I have Lupus to begin with, and that was the initial start of my kidney failure, but it was accelerated by having to carry heavy water and canned foods three and four times a day. It almost killed me."

Brittany: "It got to a point where I talked to my mom, and I told her what was going on, and she was a retired nurse, and she said there was a lot of protein being broken down by us going up and down the steps and trying to survive. She said it's not good for him, so his doctor told him the reason why it had accelerated was because of the storm. His renal doctor was shocked by how fast it happened, and David was in the hospital for a week straight and then got out."

Why is your family not helping with your homeless situation?

Brittany: "I grew up in a lot of violence. At 12 years old, I ran through automatic gunfire, and found my brother was sitting outside a window where bullets had gone through the window and wall of our house. I ran and grabbed him and took him to hide underneath the front porch. I didn't know if Mom and Dad had survived or not. My parents divorced when I was a teenager. There's a lot of negative thoughts and feelings that happened after the divorce. I've had pain since I was 13 or 14 years old, and then I got really sick at 16, and doctors put me on pain medication. I was automatically labeled a person on drugs by my family. I was no longer invited to family events and was shunned. It got back to me that they would make fun of me because I was sick and could not work. My uncle and my dad were putting that into the family, and unfortunately, it has stuck. So, when it comes to help, it is not going to come. I've tried to prove that I'm not an addict, but they say I'm faking it, even though it's a genetic condition. I love my family, but I have to love them from a distance. So, when it comes to asking for help, my mom is disabled and really sick and on a limited income, so she can't help much."

David: "My mom is on a very limited income, so she helps when she can, but she's also living with my sister, so it's hard to get anything on that side."

Brittany: "I've forgiven my family, and I hope they will accept me. I have a relationship with my dad and my mom, but it's at a distance."

Do you feel like you've run out of solutions?

David: "It kind of feels like it. We're in a hopeless spot, like this town doesn't want to help anybody."

Brittany: "I feel like from the very beginning we put in a huge amount of effort, and I have notebooks full of notes of all the places we've gone to and asked for help. We've applied, we've called, and I've stayed on top of that every single day."

David: "We've been living in a hotel for almost eight months."

Brittany: "And I feel, it's hard to fight and stay on course when you're trying to see if we're going to end up in the car today, and wondering whether I'm going to have food today or whether we'll have gas for the car today? I feel like we're still fighting really hard. Now, I'm struggling every day, nothing is coming of this, so it's hard to keep going."

David: "It's almost to the point that we've decided to leave Asheville. One of their posts was about needing to bring tourists in."

Brittany: "I've always tried to have a plan, but this has been one of the hardest for me. I've gone through a lot of crap in my life. The situation is ever-changing, and it hurts to hear 'No' every time. Am I failing? We're still in the fight. We're fighting every day.

Something that has kept us in the fight is the people that we've met. Most of the people who have helped me weren't state or federal; it's been community people. The first people who helped us were a group of people who drove from Florida and came to our apartment complex and brought us food, water, and five gallons of gas.

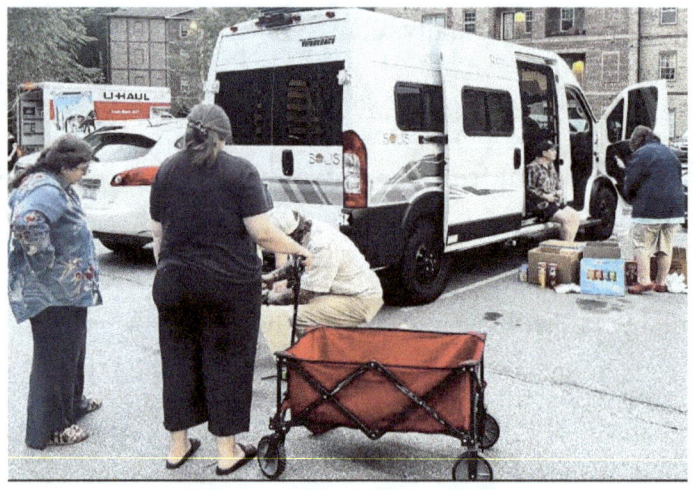

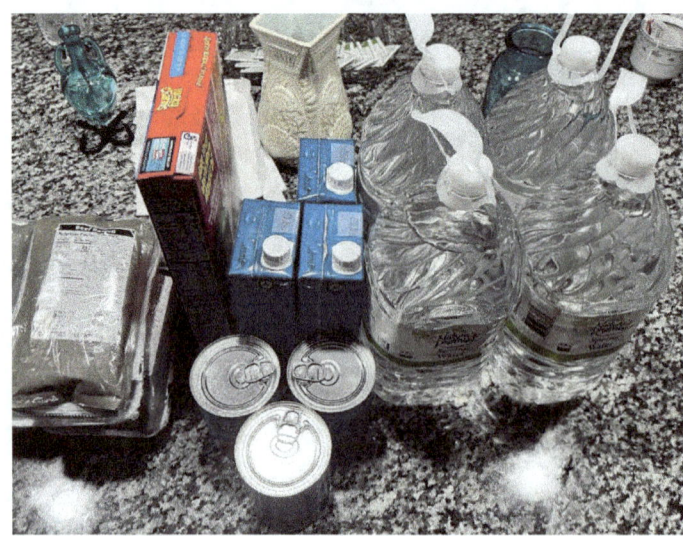

<u>How about the other neighbors at your apartment complex?</u>

Brittany: "There was a woman, a beautiful black woman, who was standing by the pool and getting water out of the swimming pool to use for toilets. We were asking her questions about whether she'd been able to get out and get money, and she said, 'I don't have to worry about getting money because I'm old-school. I keep a little bit of money on me at all times, but you guys are younger and haven't figured that out yet.' So, I asked her for some advice and she said, 'Hold on for a minute' and disappeared. We had not asked her for anything, and she walked over and gave us $60, and that was all the money that we had the entire time. We went to Ingles, stood in line for a long time, and the shelves were empty."

David: "Grocery stores were only accepting cash, and all my money was in the bank where I couldn't get to it, so we didn't have any. Plus, what money I did have, the bank took it from me because I had a loan that I owed."

Brittany: "So, throughout this whole thing, something that stands out to me is it hasn't been organizations, it hasn't been Asheville, it hasn't been Buncombe County government, there hasn't been any help."

David: "It's been the community."

Brittany: "It's been the community, the churches, the individuals that don't even know you."

David: "The ones that don't even know you."

Brittany: "They're the ones who have inspired me to keep going because without that love and care of the community, it's scary."

How do you keep going?

David: "We try to stay positive for the most part. We laugh. Some days are harder than others."

Brittany: "I think you have to have a sense of humor to get through anything that is hard. I have CPTSD (Complex Post Traumatic Stress Disorder), depression, and anxiety, and take medication. What I've learned is you have to put your head down and focus on what's most important and work towards that goal. I put that picture of me, David, and the two boys in front of me to help me keep going.

You have to let the materialistic things go and put the most important things in front of you. Don't give up. Have hope. It's important not to forget who you are and use whatever you've been through to get through this. Giving up is not an option."

I understand you have a GoFundMe account.

Brittany: "I've been sharing the link and can probably do it more, but my pain that I face on a daily basis makes it difficult to keep working on it."

David: "We try to post it every couple of days."

Brittany: "It's really hard sleeping in the car because I get really stiff. I've had to pee in a cup and go pour it out, or go to gas stations.

David: "We have to constantly move around because it's not safe to stay in one place too long."

Brittany: "There are so many other people parked in grocery store parking lots, having to park and sleep in their cars."

Reports estimate that around 1,500 people are homeless. What's your estimate?

David: "That number has to be exponentially bigger. I would say at least 3,000."

Brittany: "I would say thousands. We saw about 25 cars of homeless people parked in the parking lot. We even saw people staying in the hotel with the FEMA vouchers who were dumpster diving to feed their families."

David: "We know of at least 25 people who got booted out of the hotel when FEMA left."

Brittany: "I feel like we had more of a voice when we worked with some friends, but there was some crooked things going on behind the scenes. We were promised a camper, and it fell through, and they were putting a lot of pressure on us to do LIVE events, and we had to block them. People were using us for money. Some of the money went where it should have, but other money didn't. We've seen a lot of shady things. I hope that we find a home, even if it's temporary."

David: "I'm still fighting for my disability, and I'm still getting unemployment for the next three weeks, and then it's over."

Brittany: "I think the last check will be June 16th, and then we'll be back in the car."

David: "We've gotten messages from people asking why we can't just go back to work, but we're disabled, so we can't. If we could, we would have already been back."

Brittany: "I was working two jobs when this illness struck me down."

David: "I was working 40 hours a week."

Brittany: "If you'd ask me 10 years ago where I'd be today, I'd never have thought this. For years and years, my father ridiculed me about not being able to work

204

because of my illness. Well, a couple of years ago, he got really sick and he called me and he said, 'You know when I used to drive by homeless people on the road, I felt like they were wasted space and didn't deserve to breathe. When I would see sick people, I would think they were useless. Now that I've gotten sick and I'm older and have seen you struggle, you have taught me compassion, you've taught me how to love and to open my eyes. Now, anytime I see those people on the side of the road, I think about you and the suffering that you face.'"

What do you want people to know about homelessness?

Brittany: "I would want them to ask themselves, 'What would you do in the same situation if the tables were turned? Everything is individualistic. Every single person has a story, and their life matters, and hearing that story can change your heart, and if my dad's heart can be changed by my story, I think other people's hearts can too. All of our stories are different. I think instead of hardening our hearts to things we're not accustomed to, you have to open your heart and allow yourself to be able to feel what that other person is feeling, have that empathy, and open your heart to it. Give people a chance. We've met homeless people just like us. We've met addicts. The system is not set up to help people like it should. As humans, I think we need to be able to open our hearts. Other homeless people we've met are willing to help us."

David: "They will give the shirt off their back for you. The people who don't have anything are willing to give you everything they have."

The Weather Channel - Asheville, North Carolina

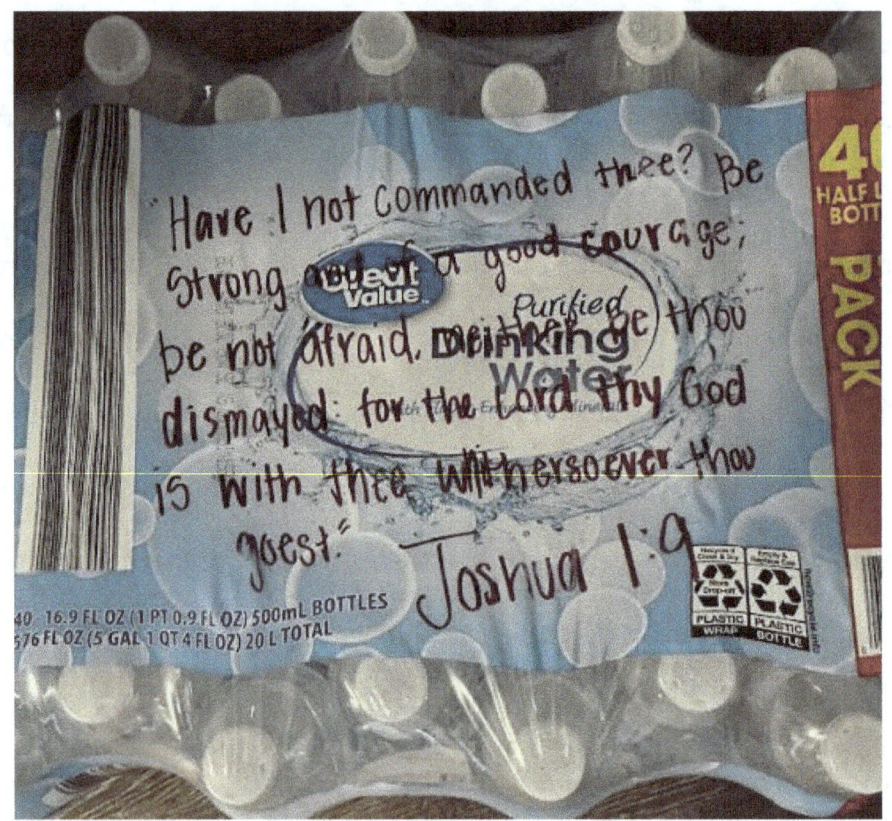

"Have I not commanded thee? Be strong and of a good courage; be not afraid, neither be thou dismayed: for the Lord thy God is with thee whithersoever thou goest." Joshua 1:9

CHAPTER FOURTEEN

Lessons & Future Preparations

"If it weren't for locals helping and volunteers, WNC families would have been screwed."

CHAPTER FOURTEEN: Lessons & Future Preparations

In my opinion, the best preparation for another natural disaster is to review what we did right and what could have been improved. Following the storm, I asked people on my social media account for any suggestions they would like to share with people facing a natural disaster.

Diana Cassara mentioned that there was a lack of shelter and government assistance: "If it weren't for locals helping and volunteers coming in with donations, Western North Carolina families would have been screwed. Some families still are. Government assistance has been minimal, and people are still in desperate need of help."

Robin Lynn Cantrell explained, "Communication with family and friends is very important in a natural disaster. The not knowing is traumatizing."

Ashley Taylor stressed the importance of "preparation and information," which she believed were equally crucial.

Kandy Sherlin Moore recounted a lesson learned from the storm: "I'm from the Emma area of Asheville. I could have gotten our pine tree cut down. I had been debating for a while. Since it was my son's first Christmas tree, it held sentimental value. He is now 37 years old. The tree had to be at least 45 or 50 years old. Plus, it was the only shade in front of the house. My husband and I were standing at the sliding glass door, discussing how we should have had the tree cut down. Suddenly, it came crashing down on the house. It destroyed the brand-new front porch we had just built, and it landed on the roof. All you could see were tree limbs. We couldn't get out the back door because there were so many tree limbs on the deck. My husband and I had been remodeling our house for 11 years. We had just worked 7 weeks straight with one day off, finishing the last room, the master bathroom. We built the new deck before we finished the master bathroom. Then the storm came the day after we finished. And we couldn't use the house for almost two months because of no water or power."

Emma area – Asheville, North Carolina

Following Hurricane Helene, I made a conscious decision to be better prepared for future storms. However, preparing for a flooding event where flooding isn't usually a problem seems impossible. Even worse is a mudslide that appears out of nowhere; however, it is best to plan for the worst-case scenario. While searching online for guidance, I located an emergency supply list created by the National Weather Service and FEMA. Based on my experience and the advice of others, I have added a few more items to the list below. I recommend that you and your family take the time to create a plan, regardless of the disaster.

1. Cash (ATMs don't work in a power outage, and gas stations will only take cash.)
2. Bottled water (1 gallon per person, per day – 3 days is recommended.)
3. Battery-operated radio or NOAA weather radio
4. Portable cell phone charger and extra cord
5. Non-perishable foods, MREs (canned goods, crackers, tuna, potted meat, chips, boxed drinks)
6. Manual can opener
7. Cooking pot
8. Plastic or paper dishes and utensils
9. Plastic trash bags
10. Aluminum foil
11. Bleach
12. Flashlight or lantern with extra batteries (candles if inside a large metal or glass container, matches)
13. Toilet wipes (Without water, you'll need to be able to clean up.)
14. Hand sanitizer and soap
15. Toothbrush and toothpaste
16. First-aid supplies (band-aids, disinfectant, ointment, gauze, rubbing alcohol, tourniquet)
17. Sunscreen and sunglasses
18. Mosquito repellent
19. Acetaminophen, antibacterial ointment, and anti-diarrhea medicine
20. Toilet tissue/paper towels
21. Trash bags (for disposal of waste if unable to flush)
22. Paper, pen/pencil, books, puzzles, card games (to help with boredom and save phone battery)
23. Sleeping bag or warm blanket (one per person in household)

24. Pet supplies (food, leash, carrier, litter, vaccination records, food and water containers)
25. Prescription medication refills
26. Non-prescription medicine (pain reliever, anti-diarrhea, antacids, laxatives)
27. Copies of insurance policies, identification, shot records, contracts, deeds, titles, passports, social security cards, and bank account records (save electronically or place in a waterproof, portable container)
28. A written list of important phone numbers
29. Complete change of clothing and sturdy shoes
30. Personal hygiene items (deodorant, cotton swabs, feminine items)
31. Prescription eyeglasses, reading glasses, contacts, contact solution
32. Whistle or flare (to signal help)
33. Ice packs and ice cooler (storage for insulin or any medicine requiring refrigeration)
34. Baby items: baby formula, diapers, wipes, bottles, baby wipes, powdered milk, blankets, extra clothes, medication, lotion)
35. Raincoat/jacket/raingear/Hat
36. Plastic tarp (for leaks)
37. Bucket or empty jugs for water collection
38. A full gas tank, a gas can, and a funnel (Some newer cars like the Ford Escape require a special funnel, which should be located with your spare tire.)
39. Generator (Place 20-25 feet away from home/windows, and must be used outdoors.)
40. Grill and charcoal (outdoor use only)
41. Fire extinguisher
42. A cooler with ice
43. Paper plates and plastic flatware
44. Dust or medical mask (helps filter contaminated air)
45. Wrench or pliers (turn off utilities)
46. Local maps
47. Ax, handsaw, pliers, screwdrivers, knife, work gloves
48. Hammer and nails (to assist with breaking through the roof)[xcix]

Additionally, a neighbor on Nextdoor.com suggested having a Go Bag, which includes the necessities and will allow you to grab and go in an emergency with little to no notice. She also mentioned "videotaping your entire home, every drawer, your garage/shed/storage facility, and outside property... not to expect your GPS to work…leave outgoing messages on your cell phone messaging system that includes your route, destination expectation and who to contact in the event you don't show up in time!"[c]

Following discussions with neighbors regarding preparing for future disasters, many said they would never be caught off guard again. Although most people have decided to remain in Western North Carolina, they have questions about the government's involvement in the events leading up to the disaster. Additionally, confusion still exists about how losing communication was so easy, given that Internet technology has existed for over 50 years. So far, no one can explain how we could have been without cell phone signals for a long time, especially when providers promised SOS calls in an emergency. Perhaps an investigation should be launched into the problems we experienced in Western North Carolina, particularly given the numerous cell phone towers.

CHAPTER FIFTEEN

Victims Lost

"Twenty people were killed in landslides, and 18 died from blunt force injuries."

CHAPTER FIFTEEN: Victims Lost

Due to privacy and legal concerns, I am unable to list the names of the victims who perished in and after Hurricane Helene. However, below is a summary of the number of people affected throughout North Carolina. Please note that this is an exhaustive list, and some individuals are still unaccounted for following the storm.

Some have asked why I decided to write a book about Helene, and my simple answer is this: I don't want to forget the victims, and I want to help prepare others for similar disasters. Without listing the names of victims, you will find a list from October 16, 2024, illustrating the North Carolina location and causes of death discovered by Helene.

Death toll listed by County:

- One in Ashe County
- Five in Avery County
- 42 in Buncombe County
- One in Burke County
- One in Catawba County
- Two in Cleveland County
- One in Gaston County
- Five in Haywood County
- Seven in Henderson County
- Two in Macon County
- Four in Madison County
- One in McDowell County
- Three in Mecklenburg County
- Two in Mitchell County
- One in Polk County
- One in Rowan County
- Three in Rutherford County
- One in Wake County
- Two in Watauga County
- One in Wilkes County
- One in Yadkin County
- 11 in Yancey County

Causes of death:

- First Responder drowned during rescue
- Motorcycle accident
- A car swept away by floodwater
- First Responder and others in a landslide
- Swannanoa River and house collapse drownings
- Swannanoa River and apartment collapse drowning
- North Toe floodwater drowning
- Green Mountain floodwater drownings
- Catawba County two-vehicle crash
- Landslide and floodwaters
- Fallen tree limb strike
- Lake Lure drownings[ci]
- Pet drownings of senior cat, Maggie Woolery, and Dog Bella *(names approved by pet owners)*

Asheville, North Carolina

Each day brings the realization that we are far from finished with the Hurricane

Helene disaster in Western North Carolina. Although Buncombe County suffered the most Helene-related deaths, the discoveries aren't over, and this may change. In the end, our main hope is that we can find everyone who is missing and bring closure to the friends and families of the victims. Drownings, landslides, blunt force injuries, and vehicle crashes took many loved ones from us, and we will never recover from the loss. Through it all, we've learned the importance of respecting our neighbors, helping those in need, and loving those who are less fortunate than ourselves. Communities put aside political divisions, and communities banded together to cope with the horrific event that changed all our lives. As we continue to deal with trauma from the storm, we do our best to heal and learn from our mistakes. A life, all lives matter, and moving forward, I pray that we continue to work together and help one another heal. *Hurricane Helene Resiliency After the Storm Part One* is only one part of the story, and more stories still need to be told.

Author's Note

The pain and fear felt by friends, neighbors, and residents of Western North Carolina have been the most poignant experience. In 53 years, nothing has ever scarred me as profoundly as seeing what Hurricane Helene has done to my home in the mountains. Not having communication with friends and family made me feel like I was in another world, centuries before the comforts of the telephone, television, and radio.

I think back on my experience in Tennessee during the Blizzard of 1993. I recall being stranded at my boyfriend's house for five days due to the storm. Those were the longest five days of my life, and that's when I realized how helpless I felt in that situation. It's ironic how a significant weather event altered the trajectory of my life. Hurricane Helene brought Western North Carolina to the depths of despair. Weather forecasters often inaccurately report storms and regularly miscalculate their severity. So, it is understandable why they did not accurately report this storm. Known for always being prepared and preaching to others about the necessity of preparation, I failed miserably to prepare for the worst two months of my life.

Never could I have prepared for the fear, shock, sadness, and helplessness that enveloped me before, during, and after Hurricane Helene. I know we will survive and become stronger following this experience, but the feelings of helplessness remain. As I sit in my warm apartment while freezing winds blow outside, and the temperatures plummet as darkness falls, I'm overcome with the unfathomable feelings of survivor's guilt. I mourn for the people who are still searching for their family members, friends, and pets who have been missing since September 27, 2024.

There are many unanswered questions, like what about the people who must live in tents and use kerosene and propane heaters for warmth? What about people who will never see their loved ones again? We took a journey through the events that unfolded on September 26, 2024. This book illustrates how people's attitudes have changed regarding storm preparation and the knowledge that has been acquired and shared about the catastrophe.

Many have asked how they can help Western North Carolina recover from the storm. If you know someone affected by the storm, please consider donating financial assistance directly to them. Some organizations that collect donations can take time to transfer the funds to families in need. However, BeLoved Asheville has been on the front lines helping communities throughout Western North Carolina. Another way to help us recover is to visit Western North Carolina. **And, best of all, a portion of the proceeds from your purchase of *Hurricane Helene Resiliency After the Storm, Part One* will help victims.**

Acknowledgments

1. Interviewees: Caron Almond, Tanya Cargo, Anjellique Collet, Richard "Rick" Spruill, Jazmin Read-Sterling, Christy Hyler, Laurrell Jackson-Smith, Kandy Sherlin Moore, Stan Sutrich, Bobby Massey, Randy Woodruff, Carrie Myers, Coley Duffie & Cody Ward, Brittany McCarson & David Beaver, and John Doe.

2. Survey Respondents: Diana Cassara, Robin Lynn Cantrell, Ashley Taylor, and Kandy Sherlin Moore.

3. Author of poem, "Sounds": Anja Woody

4. Author of poem, "These Mountains": Carrie Myers

5. Book Cover: Designed by Emmanuel Paul from Alignable.com

6. Book Trailer #1: Joshua James

7. Book Trailer #2: Emmanuel Paul

8. North Carolina photographs provided by the following individuals:
   - Michele Bretz – West Asheville
   - Laurrell Jackson-Smith – Asheville, Swannanoa
   - Bobby Massey & Randy Woodruff – Hendersonville, Arden, and Fletcher
   - Anjellique Collet - Candler
   - Rick Spruill & Chimney Rock Brewing – Chimney Rock and Lake Lure
   - Jeff Moore – Marshall
   - Tim Burleson – Stoney Fork, Candler
   - Michele Bretz - Windwood Park, Asheville
   - Amanda Davis – Burton Street, Asheville
   - Virginia Jones – Tunnel Road, Asheville
   - Caron Almond – Old Fort and Morganton
   - Kimberly Israel – River Arts District, Asheville
   - Aaron Lubeck – River Arts District, Asheville
   - Connie French – River Arts District and The Biltmore Village, Asheville
   - John Doe (Anonymous) – Swannanoa
   - Stan Sutrich – Barnardsville
   - Melvin Dreco Livingston – Tunnel Road, Asheville
   - Jack Harmon – Black Mountain

9. Survey responses from social media included Diana Cassara, Robin Lynn Cantrell, Ashley Taylor, Jazmine Read-Sterling, and Kandy Sherlin Moore.

10. **Special recognition and appreciation to:**
    a. Families and friends of those who perished during the storm. Our hearts bleed for you, and we pray that your pain will lessen as each day passes.

    b. Radio station employees who worked around the clock to provide minute-by-minute updates regarding care stations, government updates, and assistance locating loved ones missing in the storm.

    c. Sage Turner of the Asheville City Council for daily updates during and following the storm.

    d. All first responders, emergency personnel, and volunteers who risked their lives to help others and bring us hope.

    e. Our friends, neighbors, and strangers with chainsaws who cleared the way for people to escape or travel to find necessities.

Author's Additional Works

- *Hating Self by Boo Black*, including Life poem by Rebecca Phillips – autobiographical, available on Amazon.com, Barnesandnoble.com, Noir Collective, and Firestorm Books in Asheville, North Carolina.
- *Loving Self by Boo Black*, including Fearless poem by Rebecca Phillips – autobiographical, available on Amazon.com, Barnesandnoble.com, Noir Collective, and Firestorm Books in Asheville, North Carolina.
- *Butterfly Blossoms by Rachel Bleu* – adult LGBTQ fiction, available on Amazon.com, Barnesandnoble.com, Noir Collective, and Firestorm Books in Asheville, North Carolina.
- *Dragonfly Passion by Rachel Bleu* – adult LGBTQ fiction, date TBD 2026.
- Short Stories by Rebecca Wells Phillips – "Homeless Again" and "It's Only a Dream" (published on Reedsy.com) and unpublished, "The Divine Connection".
- "Appointment with the Grim Reaper" – written for author CJ Myers' book, *The Other Side of Fear*, date TBD.

Please consider writing a book review of any of Rebecca's books on Amazon, Barnes & Noble, and Goodreads. To submit questions or comments, feel free to contact the author directly at one of the following platforms:

- Email: rebeccawellsphillips@gmail.com

- Website: www.rebeccawellsphillips.com

- X (Twitter): https://x.com/RebeccaPhi37526

- TikTok: https://www.tiktok.com/@rebecca.phillips53

- Facebook: https://facebook.com/beckywellsphillips

i https://www.merriam-webster.com. "Resiliency". Merriam-Webster.com Dictionary. Oct. 20, 2024.

ii The poem was written by Anja Woody, Oct. 18, 2024.

iii www.usatoday.com, Randy Aldridge, *Top 10 Deadliest Hurricanes*, Oct. 6, 2024.

iv www.cnn.com, Ray Sanchez, *The Power of Water: How Helene Devastated Western North Carolina*, Oct. 6, 2024, 7:05 PM.

v www.wavy.com/100-years-later, Keaton Eberly and Laura Smith, Oct. 12, 2024, 8:02 AM.

vi www.carriermanagement.com and AccuWeather, *Helene Damage Numbers Climb*, Sept. 27, 2024.

vii www.cnet.com, Cierra Noffke, *Looking for Free Internet After Hurricanes Helene and Milton? You Can Still Get a Connection From These Providers,* Oct. 14, 2024, 10:00 AM PT.

viii www.citizen-times.com, Will Hofmann, *'Worst storm damage I have seen': Helene batters Fletcher, Henderson, in historic floods,* Sept. 27, 2024, updated Oct. 3, 2024, 5:52 PM ET.

ix www.foxweather.com, North Carolina Dept. of Commerce, Andrew Wulfeck, *Unemployment rate more than triples in heart of North Carolina's Hurricane Helene disaster zone,* Dec. 4, 2024 8:58 PM EST.

x www.abc11.com, WLOS, *Hurricane Helene victims live in campers, tents after their homes were destroyed by storm*, October 23, 2024, 9:07 pm.

xi www.wbtv.com, Erica Lunsford, *Nearly 50 animals evacuated from Asheville to Charlotte after flooding from Helene damaged shelter*, Oct. 2, 2024, 8:01 PM EDT.

xii www.828newsnow.com, Associated Press, Stephany Matat and Olga R. Rodriguez, *Hurricane Helene victims include family swept away in Asheville*, Oct. 2, 2024, 3:54 PM EDT.

xiii www.ncmedsoc.org and National Weather Service, Claire Fry, *Helene rain totals: How much fell in NC mountain towns?* published Sept. 28, 2024, 4:16 PM EDT, updated Sept. 28, 2024, 5:57 PM EDT.

xiv www.roadsbridges.com, ABC News, CNN, WXIN, Fox 5, *Hurricane Helene Destroys Roads and Bridges Across South*, Oct. 1, 2024.

xv www.wlos.com, Dean Hensley, *NCDOT: I-40 East reopens from Buncombe County to McDowell County near Old Fort*, Oct. 1, 2024, 2:39 PM.

xvi www.usatoday.com, Doyle Rice and Dinah Voyles Pulver, *Mountain Terrain, monstrous rain: What caused North Carolina's catastrophic flooding*, Oct. 1, 2024, 2:12 PM ET.

xvii www.knoxnews.com, Alison Kiehl, *When will Interstate 40 reopen at the Tennessee/North Carolina state line? Maybe early 2025*, published 9:15 PM ET, Nov. 5, 2024, updated 10:28 AM ET Dec. 27, 2024.

xviii www.wyff4.com, Nate Stanley, *Family's home robbed after being displaced from Hurricane Helene damage*, updated Dec. 5, 2024, 11:15 PM EST.

xix www.ncdoj.gov/attorney-general-josh-stein, Nazneen Ahmed, *Attorney General Josh Stein Provides Update on Hurricane Helene-Related Price Gouging*, Oct. 11, 2024.

xx www.citizen-times.com, Iris Seaton, *Internet outages persist after Helene: Spectrum details restoration progress, obstacles*, published Oct. 10, 2024, 11:01 AM ET, updated Oct. 12, 2024, 12:44 PM ET.

xxi www.abc11.com, CNN Wire, Taylor Thompson, WLOS, *NC Family Recounts Harrowing Escape from Rising Floodwaters During Hurricane Helene*, Oct. 20, 2024.

xxii www.ncdisaster.ces.ncsu.edu, Dr. Matt Poore, *"Helping Livestock Farmers Assess Damage from Hurricane Helene,"* updated Oct. 9, 2024.

xxiii www.elteccorp.com, April Spears, *What Should You Do If a Traffic Light Is Malfunctioning*, Mar. 9, 2021.

[xxiv] www.wral.com and PolitiFact by Paul Specht, *Fact-checking 5 misleading claims about Helene relief efforts*, published 10:57 PM Oct. 4, 2024, updated 3:46 PM Dec. 18, 2024.

[xxv] www.ncmedsoc.org, Randy Aldridge, *Gov. Roy Cooper's Latest on Helene as Others Finally Get Access to Hardest Hit Areas of WNC*, Oct. 7, 2024.

[xxvi] www.allhandsandhearts.org, *Latest Hurricane Helene Updates*, Sept. 28, 2024, 8:30 EDT, Update 15.

[xxvii] www.CNNweather.com, Dalia Faheid and Dakin Andone, *Helene flooding strands hundreds of North Carolina residents as storm's death toll reaches 95*, updated 11:06 PM EDT, Sept. 29, 2024.

[xxviii] www.PowerOutage.us, Duke Energy News Center, *Duke Energy restores power to 723,000 Carolinas customers, restoration work continues as company determines restoration times for hardest-hit areas*, Sep. 28, 2024.

[xxix] www.wtvr.com, National Weather Service, CNN Wire, *Helene flooding strands hundreds of North Carolina residents as storm's death toll reaches 93*, Sep. 29, 2024, 10:23 PM.

[xxx] www.ncdoj.gov, Nazneen Ahmed, *Attorney General Josh Stein Provides Update on Price Gouging After Hurricane Helene*, Sep. 30, 2024.

[xxxi] www.nypost.com, Zoe Hussain, *Picturesque North Carolina mountain town destroyed by Hurricane Helene as death toll surpasses 100*, published Sept. 30, 2024, updated Sept. 30, 2024, 7:33 pm.

[xxxii] www.nytimes.com, The New York Times, Eduardo Medina, Nicholas Bogel-Burroughs, Isabella Kwai and Tim Arango, *Gas, Power and Phone Outages Impede Rescues in North Carolina*, published Sept. 28, 2024, updated Oct. 1, 2024.

[xxxiii] www.ncnewsline.com, The Pulse, Brandon Kingdollar, *NC Attorney General's office received more than 100 Helene price gouging complaints*, Oct. 2, 2024, 1:27 PM.

[xxxiv] www.dailycommercial.com, USA Today Network, Ana Rocio Alverez Brinez, Fernando Cervantes Jr., Dinah Voyles Pulver, and Eduardo Cuevas, *As Lake County prepares for Milton, which are the worst hurricanes in US history*, Oct. 9, 2024, 12:38 PM ET.

[xxxv] www.AOL.com, Greenville News, Nina Tran, *Helene is one of the deadliest hurricanes to impact US. A look at past deadly hurricanes*, Oct. 4, 2024.

[xxxvi] www.Newsweek.com, Hugh Cameron, *How FEMA Funding for Helene Compares to Hurricanes Andrew, Katrina, Sandy*, published Oct. 7, 2024, 11:21 AM EDT, updated Oct. 7, 2024, 12:11 PM EDT.

[xxxvii] www.wlos.com, Jennifer Emert, *Bypass line reconnected at reservoir; efforts continue to restore Asheville water*, published Oct. 10, 2024, 9:21 AM EDT, updated Oct. 10, 2024, 6:13 PM EDT.

[xxxviii] www.thevalleyecho.com, Fred McCormick, *Black Mountain works to restore water and sanitation services*, Oct. 12, 2024.

[xxxix] www.mitchellnews.com, Randy Foster, *The lingering impacts of Helene*, published Oct. 15, 2024.

[xl] www.nextdoor.com, Sage Turner, Asheville City Council, *Daily Update*, Oct. 14, 2024.

[xli] www.aol.com, Asheville Citizen-Times, Sarah Honosky, *Non-potable water returns to nearly 95% of Asheville's system*, Oct. 21, 2024, 6:46 AM EST.

[xlii] www.nextdoor.com, Resident Sarah Gewanter posted about Marshall, North Carolina, Oct. 12, 2024.

[xliii] www.facebook.com, Facebook Group: Friends of Swannanoa, *October 18 Update*, North Carolina, posted Nov. 12, 2024.

[xliv] www.wlos.com, ABC13 News, *North Carolina's Helene death toll rises to 95, according to state*, Oct. 16, 2024, 10:26 AM, updated Oct. 17, 2024, 10:21 AM.

[xlv] www.citizen-times.com, Jacob Wilt, *How many died in North Carolina from Hurricane Helene? See county-by-county list*, published Oct. 2, 2024, 5:35 PM, updated Oct. 22, 2024, 12:29 PM.

[xlvi] www.citizen-times.com, Connor Giffin, *First lady Jill Biden stirs beans, praises volunteers in post-Helene visit to Asheville*, Oct. 25, 2024, 11:41 AM ET, updated 7:22 PM ET.

[xlvii] www.nextdoor.com, Sage Turner, Asheville City Council, *Daily Update*, Oct. 28, 2024, 8:00 PM.

[xlviii] www.nextdoor.com, Sage Turner, Asheville City Council, *Daily Update*, Nov. 2, 2024.

[xlix] www.facebook.com, Anonymous, *Hurricane Helene*, posted Nov. 4, 2024.

[l] www.nextdoor.com, Sage Turner, Asheville City Council, *Daily Update*, Nov. 6, 2024.

[li] www.nextdoor.com, Sage Turner, Asheville City Council, *Daily Update*, Nov. 8, 2024, 10:30 PM.

[lii] www.facebook.com, Laurrell Jackson-Smith, *Hurricane Helene Cleanup*, Nov. 10, 2024.

[liii] www.nextdoor.com, Sage Turner, Asheville City Council, *Daily Update*, Nov. 13, 2024.

[liv] www.nextdoor.com, Sage Turner, Asheville City Council, *Daily Update*, Nov. 14, 2024, 10:30 pm.

[lv] www.nextdoor.com, Mike Rains, *Hurricane Helene and Thanksgiving*, posted Nov. 16, 2024.

[lvi] www.nextdoor.com, Sage Turner, Asheville City Council, *Daily Update*, Nov. 21, 2024.

[lvii] www.nextdoor.com, Susan Vaughan, *Barnardsville*, posted Nov. 25, 2025.

[lviii] www.newsobserver.com, Brian Gordon, *Pensacola's battered lone road adds twists to Helene response in remote Western NC town*, published Dec. 3, 2024, 5:17 PM, updated Dec. 3, 2024, 7:03 PM.

[lix] www.gizmodo.com, Isaac Schultz, *Record-Breaking Winds and Shocking Damage: What Made 2024's Hurricanes Unforgettable*, Dec. 4, 2024.

[lx] www.citizen-times.com, Will Hofmann and Ryley Ober, *As 12,000 remain displaced from Helene, campers become homes. The problem is keeping them warm*, published Jan. 13, 2025, updated Jan. 14, 2025, 1:38 pm ET.

[lxi] www.citizen-times.com, Sarah Honosky, *BeLoved Asheville buys Swannanoa property with plans for new deeply affordable 'village'*, Published Jan. 14, 2025, 5:12 AM ET.

[lxii] www.BPRnews.com, Anna Douglas, *Persons found in Buncombe County listed as 105th fatality from Helene in North Carolina*, published Jan. 30, 2025, 3:51 PM EST.

[lxiii] www.WBTV.com, Brandy Beard, *North Carolina officials report more Hurricane Helene-related deaths months after storm*, published Feb. 12, 2025, 2:09 PM EST.

[lxiv] www.biltmorebeacon.com, The Biltmore Beacon, *Helene waterway debris removal is now underway*, Feb. 19, 2025.

[lxv] www.QueenCityNews.com, Jen Cardone, *Six months later: New analysis of Hurricane Helene reveals devastating impact*, Mar. 21, 2025.

[lxvi] www.msn.com and WNCT Greenville, Scarlett Lisjak, *Polk Co. wildfires surpass 5,700 acres, evacuations remain in place*, Mar. 21, 2025.

[lxvii] www.citizen-times.com, Todd Runkle, *Western NC wildfires updates Friday, March 28: See the latest from around the region*, Mar. 28, 2025, 10:18 AM ET.

[lxviii] www.citizen-times.com, Todd Runkle, *Western NC wildfires updates Friday, March 28: See the latest from around the region*, Mar. 28, 2025, 8:40 AM ET, updated Mar. 28, 2025, 10:18 PM.

[lxix] www.wlos.com, Dean Hensley, Marisa Sardonia, Zola Sigmon, Ruby Annas, *LIVE UPDATES (March 28): Alarka Five Fire in Swain County burns 1,300 acres*, Mar. 18, 2025, 8:28 AM, updated Mar. 28, 2025, 10:43 PM.

[lxx] www.wbtv.com, Spencer Chrisman, *Evacuation order issued in McDowell County as crews battle wildfire*, published Apr. 15, 2025, 4:54 PM EDT.

[lxxi] www.wlos.com, Marisa Sardonia, *Webb Creek Fire in Clay County reaches 45 acres, 75% contained*, Apr. 16, 2025, 11:20 AM, updated 3:45 AM.

[lxxii] www.wptf.com, Noelle Harff via UNC Media Hub, *Survive or collapse: Small businesses in North Carolina struggle after Hurricane Helene*, Oct. 29, 2025.

[lxxiii] www.tribune.com, The Express Tribune and www.facebook.com, *Candler residents dismiss rumors of 200 people stranded in church during Hurricane Helene*, Oct. 07, 2024.

[lxxiv] www.theguardian.com, Nina Lakhani, *Everything we had floated away: Hurricane Helene survivors help each other as disinformation swirls*, Feb. 16, 2025, 7:00 PM EST.

[lxxv] www.thesylvaherald.com, Dave Russell, *Dillsboro pulling together after a lashing from Helene*, Oct. 2, 2024.

[lxxvi] www.biologicaldiversity.org, Center of Biological Diversity, *Press Release: Forest Service Urged to Update N.C.'s Nantahala-Pisgah Forest Plan in Wake of Hurricane Helene*, Dec. 18, 2024.

[lxxvii] www.fox5atlanta.com, Angeli Gabriel, *Beloved 'Rainbow Bridge' in North Carolina honors lost pets washed away by Helene*, Oct. 28, 2024, 7:58 PM EDT.

[lxxviii] www.cbsnews.com, Sharyn Alfonsi, Mary Cunningham, Ashley Velie, Eliza Costas, *Helene survivors in Western North Carolina are still in shock but finding hope*, Oct. 20, 2024, 7:00 PM EDT.

[lxxix] www.spectrumlocalnews.com, Nick Buffo, *In Burnsville, focus is on rebuilding and helping neighbors*, Oct. 11, 2024, 7:38 PM EST.

[lxxx] www.highlandnews.com, News Staff, *Hard hit by Helene*, Oct. 3, 2024.

[lxxxi] www.smokymountainnews.com, Cory Vaillancourt, *Helene damage coming into focus in Waynesville*, Nov. 20, 2024.

[lxxxii] www.thesylvaherald.com, Dave Russell, *Helene: Like nothing we have ever seen in WNC*, Oct. 2, 2024.

[lxxxiii] www.facebook.com, Kimberly Wright's Post, *Straight Outta North Cove, North Carolina*, Nov. 13, 2024.

[lxxxiv] www.rivers.gov, Arthur P. Miller, Jr. and Marjorie L. Miller. *Park Ranger Guide to Rivers and Lakes: What to See and Learn on America's Freshwaters*, Stackpole Books, Harrisburg, Pennsylvania, 1991.

[lxxxv] www.davidsonflyfishing.com, Davidson River Outfitters, *Rivers and Streams of WNC: Best Fly-Fishing Rivers in Western NC*, 2025.

[lxxxvi] www.abc11.com, Julia Jacobo, *Why was the flooding in Asheville, North Carolina, so extreme?* Oct. 4, 2024.

[lxxxvii] www.usatoday.com, Eduardo Cuevas, *Infections, sewage and mosquito-borne illness outlast hurricanes*, Oct. 15, 2024, updated Oct. 22, 2024, 2:30 PM ET.

[lxxxviii] www.bestplaces.net, Best Places Staff, *Asheville, NC Cost of Living*, 2025.

[lxxxix] www.healthexec.com, Dave Fornell, *Baxter closes largest IV solution factory, sparking fears of shortage*, Oct. 3, 2024.

[xc] www.facebook.com, Laurrell Jackson-Smith, *Hurricane Helene*, posted on Oct. 17, 2024.

[xci] www.nextdoor.com, Sage Turner, Asheville City Council, *Daily Update*, Nov. 8, 2024.

[xcii] www.ashevilledailyplanet.com, From Staff Reports, *Record set as Helene more than doubles Buncombe County's homeless count*, Apr. 5, 2025.

[xciii] www.citizen-times.com, Jacob Biba, *In wake of Helene, county eyes raising property taxes to fund operations during recovery*, May 8, 2025.

[xciv] www.asheville.com, Preservation Society of Asheville and Buncombe County, *French Broad and Swannanoa River Corridors Named Among Most Endangered Historic Places*, May 8, 2025.

[xcv] www.mayoclinic.org, Mayo Clinic Staff, *Mental health: Know when to get help*, Dec. 17, 2024.

[xcvi] www.yahoo.com/news, WSOCTV.com News Staff, *Free crisis counseling, mental health resources available for Helene survivors*, Nov. 23, 2024, 1:24 PM EST.

[xcvii] www.pbs.org, Jennifer Horney and The Associated Press, *The Conversation: In mountain areas flooded by Hurricane Helene, these health risks are rising*, Oct. 2, 2024, 11:46 AM EST.

[xcviii] www.grist.com, Katie Myers and Zoya Teirstein, *As Helene's immediate impacts recede, a public health threat rises*, published Oct. 18, 2024.

[xcix] www.weather.gov, National Weather Service, Adeola Adeosun, *Emergency Supply Kit*, 2025.

[c] www.nextdoor.com, Sara C., *Hurricane Trigger Warning!!!*, May 12, 2025, 5:28 AM.

[ci] www.wlos.com, WLOS Staff, *North Carolina's Helene death toll rises to 95, according to state*, Oct. 16, 2024, 10:26 AM, updated Oct. 17, 2024, 10:21 AM.

Bibliography

ABC News. (2024, Oct. 1). *Hurricane Helene Destroys Roads and Bridges Across South.* Retrieved from Roadsbridges.com: www.roadsbridges.com

AccuWeather & Carrier Management (2024, Sept. 27). *Helene Damage Numbers Climb.* Retrieved from www.carriermanagement.com: www.carriermanagement.com

Ahmed, N. (2024, Dec. 5). *Attorney General Josh Stein Provides Update on Hurricane Helene-Related Price Gouging.* Retrieved from NCDOJ.gov: www.ncdoj.gove/attorney-general-josh-stein

Aldridge, R. (2024, Oct. 7). *Gov. Roy Cooper's Latest on Helene as Others Finally Get Access to Hardest Hit Areas of WNC.* Retrieved from NCmedsoc.org: www.ncmedsoc.org

Aldridge, R. (2024, Oct. 6). *Top 10 Deadliest Hurricanes.* Retrieved from USAtoday.com: www.usatoday.com

Alfonsi, S., Cunningham, M., Velie, A., & Costas, E. (2024, Oct. 20). *Helene survivors in Western North Carolina are still in shock but finding hope.* Retrieved from CBSnews.com: www.cbsnews.com

Brinez, A., Cervantes, Jr., F., Pulver, D.V., & Cuevas, E. (2024, Oct. 9). *As Lake County prepares for Milton, which are the worst hurricanes in US history.* Retrieved from Dailycommercial.com: www.dailycommercial.com

Andone, D. F. (2024, Sept. 29). *Helene flooding strands hundreds of North Carolina residents as storm's death toll reaches 95.* Retrieved from CNNweather.com: www.cnnweather.com

Anonymous. (2024, Nov. 4). *Hurricane Helene.* Retrieved from Facebook.com: www.facebook.com

Beacon, The Biltmore (2025, Feb. 19). *Helene waterway debris removal is now underway.* Retrieved from Biltmorebeacon.com: www.biltmorebeacon.com

Beard, B. (2025, Feb. 12). *North Carolina officials report more Hurricane Helene-related deaths months after storm.* Retrieved from WBTV.com: www.WBTV.com

Bestplaces.net. (2025, Best Places Staff). *Asheville, NC Cost of Living.* Retrieved from Bestplaces.net: www.bestplaces.net

Biba, J. (2025, May 8). *In wake of Helene, county eyes raising property taxes to fund operations during recovery.* Retrieved from Citizen-Times.com: www.citizen-times.com

Buffo, N. (2024, Oct. 11). *In Burnsville, focus is on rebuilding and helping neighbors.* Retrieved from Spectrumlocalnews.com: www.spectrumlocalnews.com

C., S. (2025, May 12). *Hurricane Trigger Warning!!!* Retrieved from Nextdoor.com: www.nextdoor.com

Cameron, H. (2024, Oct. 7). *How FEMA Funding for Helene Compares to Hurricanes Andrew, Katrina, Sandy.* Retrieved from Newsweek.com: www.newsweek.com

Cardone, J. (2025, Mar. 21). *Six months later: New analysis of Hurricane Helene reveals devastating impact.* Retrieved from QueenCityNews.com: www.queencitynews.com

Chrisman, S. (2025, Apr. 15). *Evacuation order issued in McDowell County as crews battle wildfire.* Retrieved from WBTV.com: www.wbtv.com

Citizen-Times, S. H. (2024, Oct. 21). *Non-potable water returns to nearly 95% of Asheville's system.* Retrieved from AOL.com: www.aol.com

Commerce Department & Wulfeck, A. (2024, Dec. 4). *Unemployment rate more than triples in heart of North Carolina's Hurricane Helene disaster zone.* Retrieved from Foxweather.com: www.foxweather.com

County, B. & Preservation Society of Asheville (2025, May 8). *French Broad and Swannanoa River Corridors Named Among Most Endangered Historic Places.* Retrieved from Asheville.com: www.asheville.com

Cuevas, E. (2024, Oct. 15). *Infections, sewage and mosquito-borne illness outlast hurricanes.* Retrieved from USAtoday.com: www.usatoday.com

Dean Hensley, M. S. (2025, Mar. 18). *LIVE UPDATES (March 28): Alarka Five Fire in Swain County burns 1,300 acres.* Retrieved from WLOS.com: www.wlos.com

Diversity, Biological (2024, Dec. 18). *Press Release: Forest Service Urged to Update N.C.'s Nantahala-Pisgah Forest Plan in Wake of Hurricane Helene.* Retrieved from Biologicaldiversity.org: www.biologicaldiversity.org

Douglas, A. (2025, Jan. 30). *Persons found in Buncombe County listed as 105th fatality from Helene in North Carolina.* Retrieved from BPRnews.com: www.BPRnews.com

Emert, J. (2024, Oct. 10). *Bypass line reconnected at reservoir, efforts continue to restore Asheville water.* Retrieved from WLOS.com: www.wlos.com

Energy, Duke. (2024, Sept. 28). *Duke Energy restores power to 723,000 Carolinas customers, restoration work continues as company determines restoration times for hardest-hit areas.* Retrieved from PowerOutage.us: www.PowerOutage.us

Faheid, D. & And one, D. (2024, Sept. 29). *Helene flooding strands hundreds of North Carolina residents as storm's death toll reaches 93*. Retrieved from WTVR.com: www.wtvr.com

Fornell, D. (2024, Oct. 3). *Baxter closes largest IV solution factory, sparking fears of shortage*. Retrieved from Healthexec.com: www.healthexec.com

Foster, R. (2024, Oct. 15). *The lingering impacts of Helene*. Retrieved from Mitchellnews.com: www.mitchellnews.com

Friends of Swannanoa Facebook Group (2024, Nov. 12). *October 18 Update*. Retrieved from Facebook.com: www.Facebook.com

Fry, C. & National Weather Service (2024, Sept. 28). *Helene rain totals: How much fell in NC mountain towns?* Retrieved from NCmedsoc.org: www.ncmedsoc.org

Gabriel, A. (2024, Oct. 28). *Beloved 'Rainbow Bridge' in North Carolina honors lost pets washed away by Helene*. Retrieved from Fox5atlanta.com: www.fox5atlanta.com

Gewanter, S. (2024, Oct. 12). *Marshall, North Carolina*. Retrieved from Nextdoor.com: www.nextdoor.com

Giffin, C. (2024, Oct. 25). *First Lady Jill Biden stirs beans, praises volunteers in post-Helene visit to Asheville*. Retrieved from Citizen-Times.com: www.Citizen-Times.com

Gordon, B. (2024, Dec. 3). *Pensacola's battered lone road adds twists to Helene response in remote Western NC town*. Retrieved from Newsobserver.com: www.newsobserver.com

Harff, N. (2024, Oct. 29). *Survive or collapse: Small businesses in North Carolina struggle after Hurricane Helene*. Retrieved from WPTF.com: www.wptf.com

Hearts, A. H. (2024, Sept. 28). *Latest Hurricane Helene Updates*. Retrieved from Allhandsandhearts.org: www.allhandsandhearts.org

Hensley, D. (2024, Oct. 1). *NCDOT: I-40 East reopens from Buncombe County to McDowell County near Old Fort*. Retrieved from WLOS.com: www.wlos.com

Hofmann, W. (2024, Sept. 27). *'Worst storm damage I have seen': Helene batters Fletcher, Henderson, in historic floods*. Retrieved from Citizens-Times.com: www.citizen-times.com

Honosky, S. (2025, Jan. 14). *BeLoved Asheville buys Swannanoa property with plans for new deeply affordable 'village'*. Retrieved from Citizen-Times.com: www.citizen-times.com

Horney, J. & Press, A. (2024, Oct. 2). *The Conversation: In mountain areas flooded by Hurricane Helene, these health risks are rising.* Retrieved from PBS.org: www.pbs.org

Hussain, Z. (2024, Sept. 30). *Picturesque North Carolina mountain town destroyed by Hurricane Helene as death toll surpasses 100.* Retrieved from NYpost.com: www.nypost.com

Jackson-Smith, L. (2024, Oct. 17). *Hurricane Helene.* Retrieved from Facebook.com: www.facebook.com

Jackson-Smith, L. (2024, Nov. 10). *Hurricane Helene Cleanup.* Retrieved from Facebook.com: www.facebook.com

Jacobo, J. (2024, Oct. 4). *Why was the flooding in Asheville, North Carolina so extreme?* Retrieved from ABC11.com: www.abc11.com

Kiehl, A. (2024, Nov. 5). *When will Interstate 40 reopen at the Tennessee/North Carolina state line? Maybe early 2025.* Retrieved from Knoxnews.com: www.knoxnews.com

King, K. (2024, May 23). *Recovery program that could have funded 1,000 temporary housing trailers bought 6.* Retrieved from wlos.com: www.wlos.com

Kingdollar, B. & The Pulse (2024, Oct. 2). *NC Attorney General's office received more than 100 Helene price gouging complaints.* Retrieved from NCnewsline.com: www.ncnewsline.com

Lakhani, N. (2025, Feb. 16). *Everything we had floated away: Hurricane Helene survivors help each other as disinformation swirls.* Retrieved from Theguardian.com: www.theguardian.com

Lisjak, S. & WNCT Greenville (2025, Mar. 21). *Polk Co. wildfires surpass 5,700 acres, evacuations remain in place.* Retrieved from MSN.com: www.msn.com

Lunsford, E. (2024, Oct. 2). *Nearly 50 animals evacuated from Asheville to Charlotte after flooding from Helene damaged shelter.* Retrieved from WBTV.com: www.wbtv.com

McCormick, F. (2024, Oct. 12). *Black Mountain works to restore water and sanitation services.* Retrieved from TheValleyEcho.com: www.thevalleyecho.com

Medina, E., Bogel-Burroughs, N., Kwai, I., & Arango, T. (2024, Oct. 1). *Gas, Power and Phone Outages Impede Rescues in North Carolina.* Retrieved from NYTimes.com: www.nytimes.com

Miller, A. & Miller, M. (1991). *Park Ranger Guide to Rivers and Lakes: What to See and Learn on America's Freshwaters, Stackpole Books, Harrisburg, Pennsylvania.* Retrieved from Rivers.gov: www.rivers.gov

News, ABC13. (2024, Oct. 16). *North Carolina's Helene death toll rises to 95, according to state.* Retrieved from WLOS.com: www.wlos.com

Noffke, C. (2024, Oct. 14). *Looking for Free Internet After Hurricanes Helene and Milton? You Can Still Get a Connection From These Providers.* Retrieved from www.cnet.com: www.cnet.com

Ober, W. H. (2025, Jan. 13). *As 12,000 remain displaced from Helene, campers become homes. The problem is keeping them warm.* Retrieved from Citizen-Times.com: www.citizen-times.com

Outfitters, D. R. (2025). *Rivers and Streams of WNC: Best Fly Fishing Rivers in Western NC.* Retrieved from Davidsonflyflishing.com: www.davidsonflyfishing.com

Poore, D. M. (2024, Oct. 9). *Helping Livestock Farmers Assess Damage from Hurricane Helene.* Retrieved from NCdisaster.edu: www.ncdisaster.ces.ncsu.edu

Pulver, D. & Rice, D. (2024, Oct. 1). *Mountain Terrain, monstrous rain: What caused North Carolina's catastrophic flooding.* Retrieved from USAtoday.com: www.usatoday.com

Rains, M. (2024, Nov. 16). *Hurricane Helene and Thanksgiving.* Retrieved from Nextdoor.com: www.nextdoor.com

Reports, S. (2025, Apr. 5). *Record set as Helene more than doubles Buncombe County's homeless count.* Retrieved from Ashevilledailyplanet.com: www.ashevilledailyplanet.com

Runkle, T. (2025, Mar. 28). *Western NC wildfires updates Friday, March 28: See the latest from around the region.* Retrieved from Citizen-Times.com: www.citizen-times.com

Russell, D. (2024, Oct. 2). *Dillsboro pulling together after a lashing from Helene.* Retrieved from Thesylvaherald.com: www.thesylvaherald.com

Russell, D. (2024, Oct. 2). *Helene: Like nothing we have ever seen in WNC.* Retrieved from Thesylvaherald.com: www.thesylvaherald.com

Sanchez, R. (2024, Oct. 6). *The Power of Water: How Helene Devastated Western North Carolina.* Retrieved from CNN.com: www.cnn.com

Sardonia, M. (2025, Apr. 16). *Webb Creek Fire in Clay County reaches 45 acres, 75% contained.* Retrieved from WLOS.com: www.wlos.com

Schultz, I. (2024, Dec. 4). *Record-Breaking Winds and Shocking Damage: What Made 2024's Hurricanes Unforgettable*. Retrieved from Gizmodo.com: www.gizmodo.com

Seaton, I. (2024, Oct. 10). *Internet outages persist after Helene: Spectrum details restoration progress, obstacles*. Retrieved from Citizen-Times.com: www.citizen-times.com

Service, N. & Adeosun, A. (2025). *Emergency Supply Kit*. Retrieved from Weather.gov: www.weather.gov

Smith, L. & Eberly, K. (2024, Oct. 12). *100 Years Later*. Retrieved from Wavy.com: www.wavy.com/100-years-later

Spears, A. (2021, Mar. 9). *What Should You Do If a Traffic Light is Malfunctioning*. Retrieved from Elteccorp.com: www.elteccorp.com

Specht, P. & PolitiFact (2024, Oct. 4). *Fact-checking 5 misleading claims about Helene relief efforts*. Retrieved from WRAL.com: www.wral.com

Staff, M. C. (2024, Dec. 17). *Mental health: Know when to get help*. Retrieved from Mayoclinic.org: www.mayoclinic.org

Staff, N. (2024, Oct. 3). *Hard hit by Helene*. Retrieved from Highlandnews.com: www.highlandnews.com

Staff, W. (2024, Oct. 16). *North Carolina's Helene death toll rises to 95, according to state*. Retrieved from WLOS.com: www.wlos.com

Staff, W. N. (2024, Nov. 23). *Free crisis counseling, mental health resources available for Helene survivors*. Retrieved from Yahoo.com: www.yahoo.com/news

Stanley, N. (2024, Dec. 5). *Family's home robbed after being displaced from Hurricane Helene damage*. Retrieved from WYFF4.com: www.wyff4.com

Stephany Matat, O. R. (2024, Oct. 2). *Hurricane Helene victims include family swept away in Asheville*. Retrieved from 828newsnow.com: www.828newsnow.com

Swannanoa, F. o. (2024, Nov. 12). *Swannanoa, North Carolina*. Retrieved from Facebook.com: www.facebook.com

Teirstein, Z. & Myers, K. (2024, Oct. 18). *As Helene's immediate impacts recede, a public health threat rises*. Retrieved from Grist.com: www.grist.com

Tran, N. & Greenville News (2024, Oct. 4). *Helene is one of the deadliest hurricanes to impact US. A look at past deadly hurricanes*. Retrieved from AOL.com: www.aol.com

Tribune & Facebook (2024, Oct. 7). *Candler residents dismiss rumors of 200 people stranded in church during Hurricane Helene*. Retrieved from Tribune.com: www.tribune.com

Turner, S. & Asheville City Council (2024, Oct. - Nov. 6). *Daily Update*. Retrieved from Nextdoor.com: www.nextdoor.com

Vaillancourt, C. (2024, Nov. 20). *Helene damage coming into focus in Waynesville*. Retrieved from Smokymountainnews.com: www.smokymountainnews.com

Vaughan, S. (2024, Nov. 25). *Barnardsville*. Retrieved from Nextdoor.com: www.nextdoor.com

Webster, N. W. (2024, Oct. 20). *Definitions*. Retrieved from Merriam-Webster.com: http://www.merriam-webster.com

Wilt, J. (2024, Oct. 2). *How many died in North Carolina from Hurricane Helene? See county-by-county list*. Retrieved from Citizen-Times.com: www.citizen-times.com

WLOS. (2024, Oct. 23). *Hurricane Helene victims live in campers, tents after their homes were destroyed by storm*. Retrieved from ABC11.com: www.abc11.com

WLOS, T. T. (2024, Oct. 20). *NC Family Recounts Harrowing Escape from Rising Floodwaters During Hurricane Helene*. Retrieved from ABC11.com: www.abc11.com

Woody, A. (2024, Oct. 18). *Sounds*. Asheville, NC, USA.

Wright, K. (2024, Nov. 13). *Straight Outta North Cove, North Carolina*. Retrieved from Facebook.com: www.facebook.com